I0441968

S. HRG. 114–86

BUILDING A MORE SECURE CYBER FUTURE: EXAMINING PRIVATE SECTOR EXPERIENCE WITH THE NIST FRAMEWORK

HEARING

BEFORE THE

COMMITTEE ON COMMERCE, SCIENCE, AND TRANSPORTATION UNITED STATES SENATE

ONE HUNDRED FOURTEENTH CONGRESS

FIRST SESSION

FEBRUARY 4, 2015

Printed for the use of the Committee on Commerce, Science, and Transportation

U.S. GOVERNMENT PUBLISHING OFFICE

96–958 PDF   WASHINGTON : 2015

For sale by the Superintendent of Documents, U.S. Government Publishing Office
Internet: bookstore.gpo.gov   Phone: toll free (866) 512–1800; DC area (202) 512–1800
Fax: (202) 512–2104   Mail: Stop IDCC, Washington, DC 20402–0001

CONTENTS

IV

BUILDING A MORE SECURE CYBER FUTURE: EXAMINING PRIVATE SECTOR EXPERIENCE WITH THE NIST FRAMEWORK

WEDNESDAY, FEBRUARY 4, 2015

U.S. SENATE,
COMMITTEE ON COMMERCE, SCIENCE, AND TRANSPORTATION,
Washington, DC.

The Committee met, pursuant to notice, at 9:59 a.m. in room SR–253, Russell Senate Office Building, Hon. John Thune, Chairman of the Committee, presiding.

Present: Senators Thune [presiding], Blunt, Ayotte, Moran, Gardner, Daines, Nelson, Cantwell, Klobuchar, Blumenthal, Schatz, Udall, and Peters.

OPENING STATEMENT OF HON. JOHN THUNE, U.S. SENATOR FROM SOUTH DAKOTA

The CHAIRMAN. This hearing will come to order.

Good morning and welcome.

We are here today to examine the private sector's experience working with the National Institute of Standards and Technology to develop and utilize the Framework for Improving Critical Infrastructure Cybersecurity and also to look forward to additional steps that can be taken to help improve our Nation's cybersecurity.

No country, company, or consumer is immune to cybersecurity threats. The United States faces a growing array of threats from hackers, from criminals, terrorists, and nation states who seek to gain access to sensitive or classified information. This also includes efforts to steal intellectual property or consumers' personal information, deny the availability of normally accessible online services, or potentially sabotage the networks and control systems of critical infrastructure.

While cyber threats are not new, we saw a number of notable cyber events last year. In 2014, security flaws such as Sandworm, Shellshock, POODLE, and Heartbleed compromised millions of servers and systems. Attacks on point of sale systems sent ripples through the retail industry, not to mention the significant cyber hack of Sony Pictures.

In 2014, after a decade without passage of major cybersecurity legislation, Congress passed five cybersecurity bills that were signed into law. I am especially pleased that our committee's work on the Cybersecurity Enhancement Act of 2014, which I worked on with former Chairman Rockefeller, was one of those bills the President signed into law.

(1)

Our Committee's bill ensures the continuation of a voluntary and industry-led process for identifying cybersecurity standards and best practices for critical infrastructure, codifying elements of the successful process that NIST undertook to create its Cybersecurity Framework and ensuring NIST's continued involvement in this public-private collaboration.

The law also included important provisions for research and development, workforce development, and increased public awareness. It will help to protect the public and private sectors against the growing number of cyber threats from around the world by, among other things, strengthening and directing better cooperation across Federal agencies in research and development, improving our test beds and cloud computing security, and authorizing the National Science Foundation's successful Cybercorps scholarships.

I am proud to note that Dakota State University in my home state is a leading institution of higher education in the area of cybersecurity. I appreciate that Dr. Josh Pauli, an Associate Professor of Cyber Security at DSU, has provided written remarks discussing that work, and I will submit those as a part of the record.

I called today's hearing primarily to hear from stakeholders about their experience with the NIST Framework. Released almost one year ago today, the Framework provides a common language regarding security issues to facilitate discussions within a company between the technical IT security managers and senior management. While the Framework targets organizations that own or operate critical infrastructure, businesses across all sectors may find use of the Framework beneficial.

The success of the Framework thus far is due in large part to NIST's collaborative relationship and engagement with the private sector. As a non-regulatory agency dedicated to promoting U.S. innovation and industrial competitiveness in ways that enhance economic security, NIST has been a genuine partner and has successfully combined its technical expertise in standards with the know-how of the private sector to help advance the Nation's technology infrastructure.

Congress is now tasked with important questions about what actions the Federal Government should take next. Included among those questions is: one, how do we assess the effectiveness of the Framework going forward? What incentives do businesses and consumers need to improve their cyber defenses? What type of cyber threat information sharing legislation is needed to help industry defend against more sophisticated cyber attacks? What should we do to better secure our supply chain? And what more can be done in related areas?

These questions are relevant to both the private and public sectors. According to the U.S. Government Accountability Office, "Federal agencies have significant weaknesses in information security controls . . ." Last year, I along with Senator Rockefeller sent letters to every agency under our committee's jurisdiction asking targeted questions about the measures being taken to protect systems using unsupported operating systems, as well as compliance with the Federal Information Security Management Act. As chairman, I will be continuing to conduct such oversight of agencies' information security management.

While I am pleased that Congress took a positive step to improving our cybersecurity posture by passing a number of bills in December, I believe an absolutely missing piece for this Congress is finally passing legislation to spur greater cyber threat information sharing. It is my hope that the Senate can find a path forward in this area soon. The hearing being held today underscores the seriousness of the threat and our commitment to passing information sharing legislation that did not get done in the last Congress.

I now yield to my distinguished Ranking Member, the Senator from Florida, Senator Nelson.

STATEMENT OF HON. BILL NELSON,
U.S. SENATOR FROM FLORIDA

Senator NELSON. Thank you, Mr. Chairman. And that is music to my ears because that is exactly what we need, greater sharing, because cyber attacks and data breaches have real consequences on the lives of everyday Americans. They are painful for the American family that has to juggle their responsibilities while trying to replace their credit card or get back the money that was taken from them because of a compromised bank account, or reclaim his or her identity, which is a nightmare when it gets stolen.

And they are costly for businesses that have been hacked. The estimate for Sony is something like $100 million. Some studies estimate that cyber attacks are costing American business as much as $400 billion a year. That is extraordinary. I see you nodding your head; I want you to testify about that.

These cyber attacks also threaten the national security. Now, if a saboteur came and blew up an electric plant here, that would be an attack upon America. Well, a cyber attack can do the same thing. And it is coming whether it is in the form of an electrical plant or a business grid, or a water system—whatever is going to try to inject economic pain and terror into the American people. Those attacks are upon us right now, and sooner or later, they are going to be successful. So it is not a question of if. It is a question of when is the attack going to be successful like it was with Sony.

Now, fortunately, we have got some things on our side. Everybody's awareness is being heightened. We have got a great National Institute of Standards and Technology that is constantly working. You mentioned the stuff in your home state. NIST just had their Cybersecurity Framework Workshop down in my state.

We have really got to figure out how we are going to come together, whether it be entirely voluntarily or whether there be some kind of mandate, because the necessity for all of us coming together, both government and the private sector, is upon us because of the threat to our way of life and our standard of living.

And so, Mr. Chairman, thank you. I take this very seriously. I had the privilege of serving as the Chairman of the Subcommittee in Armed Services, where I just came from, called Emerging Threats, which has as its jurisdiction cybersecurity and the national security interests. I am, needless to say, quite interested in this subject, and I appreciate your attention in calling this hearing.

The CHAIRMAN. Thank you, Senator Nelson. You are right. This has some tremendous national security implications, not to mention the enormous economic harm that you alluded to and the impact that can have on our country's economic interests.

We have a great panel with us today. We look forward to hearing from them. First off is going to be Dr. Charles Romine. He is the Director of the Information Technology Laboratory at the National Institute of Standards and Technology under the U.S. Department of Commerce. That is a long thing to put on a business card right there.

Ms. Ann Beauchesne. Ms. Beauchesne is the Vice President of National Security & Emergency Preparedness at the United States Chamber of Commerce.

Dr. Paul Smocer. Mr. Smocer is the President of BITS, the Technology Policy Division of the Financial Services Roundtable.

Mr. Jefferson England. Mr. England is the Chief Financial Officer for Silver Star Communications.

And Dr. James Lewis. Dr. Lewis is the Director and Senior Fellow of the Strategic Technologies Program at the Center for Strategic and International Studies, CSIS.

So we will look forward to hearing from all of you. We will start at my left and your right with Dr. Romine.

STATEMENT OF DR. CHARLES H. ROMINE, DIRECTOR, INFORMATION TECHNOLOGY LABORATORY, NATIONAL INSTITUTE OF STANDARDS AND TECHNOLOGY, U.S. DEPARTMENT OF COMMERCE

Dr. ROMINE. Thank you, Chairman Thune, Ranking Member Nelson, and members of the Committee. I am Dr. Charles Romine, the Director of the Information Technology Laboratory at NIST. Thank you for the opportunity to appear before you today to discuss our work in cybersecurity.

NIST has worked in cybersecurity with Federal agencies, industry, and academia since 1972. Our role to research, develop, and deploy information security standards and technology to protect information systems against threats to the confidentiality, integrity, and availability of information and services was strengthened through the Computer Security Act of 1987, broadened through the Federal Information Security Management Act of 2002, and reaffirmed in the Federal Information Security Modernization Act of 2014. The Cybersecurity Enhancement Act of 2014 also authorizes NIST to facilitate and support the development of voluntary, industry-led cybersecurity standards and best practices for critical infrastructure.

NIST accomplishes its mission in cybersecurity through collaborative partnerships with our national and international stakeholders in industry, government, academia, standards bodies, and consortia.

A prime example of these collaborations is the Framework for Improving Critical Infrastructure Cybersecurity, or just the Framework, in response to Executive Order 13636. The Framework consists of standards, guidelines, and practices to promote the protection of critical infrastructure. The prioritized, flexible, repeatable, and cost-effective approach of the Framework helps owners and operators of critical infrastructure align their policies, technologies, and day-to-day business operations to better protect their data and their information technology and industrial control systems and tailor it to individual needs.

The fact that the Framework is and will remain voluntary allows us to bring the maximum number of stakeholders to the table.

The Framework was always designed to be a living document, shaped by the experiences of those using it. Based on recent feedback, I would like to share some thoughts about where we are now almost a year since the release of the Framework.

Organizations are using the Framework in a variety of ways, such as raising awareness within their organization, including with executive leadership, improving communications of cybersecurity expectations with business partners, suppliers, and across and among sectors, and demonstrating alignment with standards, guidelines, and best practices. We have been encouraged by seeing expanding networks within and across sectors of the economy utilizing the Framework, making it more relevant to their stakeholders.

For example, technology companies are developing products and services tied to the Framework. The auditing community is leveraging the Framework to provide a consistent auditable standard, and many states are leveraging the Framework to improve the security of their critical infrastructure.

As the Framework incorporates globally recognized standards for cybersecurity, it is also serving as a model for other countries.

Current feedback indicates widespread agreement that it is too early to update the Framework. Waiting will allow for tools and services to be built and implemented. In the meantime, NIST will continue the open, transparent, and inclusive process as it considers producing guidance on the challenging aspects of implementation. NIST will work on areas singled out by the Roadmap for Improving Critical Infrastructure Cybersecurity and will continue exploring options for future governance of the Framework, understanding the benefits of this being a private sector-maintained process in the future.

NIST recognizes our essential role in helping industry, consumers, and government manage cybersecurity risks. We are extremely proud of our role in establishing and improving the comprehensive set of cybersecurity technical solutions, standards, guidelines, and best practices and the robust collaborations with our Federal Government partners, private sector collaborators, and international colleagues.

But there is still much to do. A sustained dialogue between government and the private sector is critical to ensuring we can respond to those growing challenges, and we appreciate the support of the Committee in this effort.

Thank you for the opportunity to testify today on NIST's work in cybersecurity, and I would be happy to answer any questions you may have.

[The prepared statement of Dr. Romine follows:]

PREPARED STATEMENT OF DR. CHARLES H. ROMINE, DIRECTOR, INFORMATION TECHNOLOGY LABORATORY, NATIONAL INSTITUTE OF STANDARDS AND TECHNOLOGY, UNITED STATES DEPARTMENT OF COMMERCE

Introduction

Chairman Thune, Ranking Member Nelson and Members of the Committee, I am Dr. Charles Romine, the Director of the Information Technology Laboratory (ITL) at the Department of Commerce's National Institute of Standards and Technology (NIST). Thank you for the opportunity to appear before you today to discuss NIST's work in cybersecurity.

The Role of NIST in Cybersecurity

With programs focused on national priorities from the Smart Grid and electronic health records to forensics, atomic clocks, advanced nanomaterials, and computer chips and more, NIST's overall mission is to promote U.S. innovation and industrial competitiveness by advancing measurement science, standards, and technology in ways that enhance economic security and improve the quality of life.

In the area of cybersecurity, NIST has worked with Federal agencies, industry, and academia since 1972, starting with the development of the Data Encryption Standard, when the potential commercial benefit of this technology became clear. NIST's role, to research, develop and deploy information security standards and technology to protect the Federal Government's information systems against threats to the confidentiality, integrity and availability of information and services, was strengthened through the Computer Security Act of 1987 (Public Law 100–235), broadened through the Federal Information Security Management Act of 2002 (FISMA; 44 U.S.C. § 3541[1]) and recently reaffirmed in the Federal Information Security Modernization Act of 2014 (Public Law 113–283). Importantly, the Cybersecurity Enhancement Act of 2014 (Public Law 113–274) authorizes NIST to facilitate and support the development of voluntary, industry-led cybersecurity standards and best practices for critical infrastructure—consistent with NIST's role in implementation of Executive Order 13636, "Improving Critical Infrastructure Cybersecurity".

NIST accomplishes its mission in cybersecurity through collaborative partnerships with its customers and stakeholders in industry, government, academia, standards bodies, consortia and international partners.

NIST Engagement with Industry

Beyond NIST's responsibilities under FISMA, under the provisions of the National Technology Transfer and Advancement Act (PL 104–113) and related OMB Circular A–119, NIST is tasked with the key role of encouraging and coordinating Federal agency use of voluntary consensus standards and participation in the development of relevant standards, as well as promoting coordination between the public and private sectors in the development of standards and in conformity assessment activities. NIST works with other agencies, such as the Department of State, to coordinate standards issues and priorities with the private sector through consensus standards organizations such as the American National Standards Institute (ANSI), the International Organization for Standardization (ISO), the Institute of Electrical and Electronics Engineers (IEEE), the Internet Engineering Task Force (IETF), and the International Telecommunications Union (ITU).

Partnership with industry to develop, maintain, and implement voluntary consensus standards related to cybersecurity best ensures the interoperability, security and resiliency of the global infrastructure needed to make us all more secure. It also allows this infrastructure to evolve in a way that embraces both security and innovation—allowing a market to flourish to create new types of secure products for the benefit of all Americans.

NIST believes further development of cybersecurity standards will be needed to improve the security and resiliency of critical U.S. information and communication infrastructure. The availability of cybersecurity standards and associated conformity assessment schemes is essential in these efforts, which NIST supports to help enhance the deployment of sound security solutions and build trust among those creating and those using the solutions throughout the country.

Cybersecurity Framework: Current Status

Almost one year ago, NIST issued The Framework for Improving Critical Infrastructure Cybersecurity (Framework) in accordance with Section 7 of Executive Order 13636, "Improving Critical Infrastructure Cybersecurity" (Executive Order).

---

[1] FISMA was enacted as Title III of the E-Government Act of 2002 (Public Law 107–347; 116 Stat. 2899).

The Framework, created through collaboration between industry and government, consists of standards, guidelines, and practices to promote the protection of critical infrastructure. The prioritized, flexible, repeatable, and cost-effective approach of the Framework helps owners and operators of critical infrastructure to manage cybersecurity-related risk.

Executive Order 13636 was designed to increase protection across the full range of Critical Infrastructure—those systems and assets that the Nation's economic and national security rely upon. Under Executive Order 13636, Federal Government security agencies were charged to increase the flow of valuable threat information to industry, and NIST was charged to play a convener and facilitator role in supporting the private sector's efforts to develop the Cybersecurity Framework.

The goal of the Framework is to help organizations align their policies, technologies, and day-to-day business operations to better protect their data and their information technology (IT) and industrial control systems.

The Framework also was designed to assess the capacity of the market to deliver better cybersecurity protection. During the development process for the Framework, NIST asked industry to contribute ideas about what standards, guidelines, and best practices could be used more widely to better manage cybersecurity risks, and then what steps should be taken to develop the next set of tools in these public-private partnerships.

In the course of developing the Framework document published in February of 2014, NIST estimates that more than 3,000 people from industry, academia, and government came to participate in workshops and webinars, while providing hundreds of detailed comments on drafts. The NIST approach was premised on the understanding that a Framework designed by industry would gain greater adoption throughout the private sector, and could support a vibrant market for IT security products and services.

The result of this effort is a dynamic tool that has two main parts.

First, the Framework is a collection of existing standards and best practices that proved to be helpful in protecting systems from cyber threats and ensuring business confidentiality, while protecting individual privacy and civil liberties.

Second, the Framework sets out basic guidelines that organizations can use in adopting those practices, providing them with a coherent structure to consider the many, varied approaches to cybersecurity that have proliferated in recent years.

NIST heard over and over that a key challenge facing information security professionals, senior business leaders, and company executives and boards of directors striving to address cybersecurity, was the lack of a common vocabulary and approach. As a result, the Framework starts with general guidance, and cascades to the more technical and specific, to help facilitate that dialogue with and within an organization.

The fact that the Framework is—and will remain—voluntary has allowed NIST to continue to bring the maximum number of stakeholders to the table. And the inherent flexibility of the Framework allows each organization to tailor it to individual needs.

Since the release of the Framework, NIST has strengthened its collaboration with critical infrastructure owners and operators, industry leaders, government partners, and other stakeholders to raise awareness about the Framework, encourage use by organizations across and supporting the critical infrastructure, and develop implementation guides and resources.

NIST, along with its partners across government, has focused on building on that initial awareness and on working arm-in-arm with the private sector as the Framework begins to be used within organizations, and as those organizations develop supporting products and services.

The Framework was designed to be a "living" document, shaped by the experiences of those using it. To learn more about these experiences, NIST released a Request for Information (RFI)[2] on August 26, 2014, and held its 6th Cybersecurity Framework Workshop at the University of South Florida in Tampa, Florida, on October 29 and 30, 2014. Responses to the RFI came from industry, academia and government organizations at multiple levels, as well as organizations representing large constituencies and key stakeholders in critical infrastructure sectors.

Based on that feedback, and NIST's continued work, I'd like to share some thoughts about where NIST is now—almost a year since the release of the Framework.

NIST found that organizations are using the Framework in a variety of ways. Many users have found the Framework helpful in raising awareness and commu-

---

[2]RFI—Experience with the Framework for Improving Critical Infrastructure Cybersecurity, August 26, 2014, *https://federalregister.gov/a/2014-20315*

nicating with stakeholders within their organization, including executive leadership. It is also being used to improve communications across organizations, allowing cybersecurity expectations to be shared with business partners, suppliers, and among sectors. The Framework is being used to demonstrate alignment with standards, guidelines, and best practices. The Framework is also being used as a strategic planning tool to assess risks and current practices.

In addition to those "users," we have been encouraged by seeing expanding networks—within and across sectors of the economy—beginning to learn about and take advantage of the Framework, making it more relevant to their stakeholders. This includes:

- Technology companies have been developing products and services aligned with the Framework.
- Communities of interest and associations have been sharing practical advice to help organizations to optimize their use of the Framework.
- The auditing community has begun to leverage the Framework to provide a consistent auditable standard.
- Major insurance providers have begun to offer policies tied to the Framework and are promoting it among their policy-holders.
- States have begun to leverage the Framework to improve the security of their infrastructure, including as a foundation for their work in cybersecurity for state emergency management agencies.

And, in part because the Framework incorporates globally recognized voluntary standards for cybersecurity, it is serving as a model for other countries, allowing them to match their business' perspectives with their governments' needs. In other words, this is not a "U.S.-only" Framework.

Cybersecurity Framework: Next Steps

NIST is continuing its outreach and awareness program through discussions with international partners, global companies and other interested governments, while NIST continues the primary outreach efforts to U.S. industries and organizations. This includes outreach to regulatory agencies, to facilitate a consistent understanding of the Framework across the Federal Government, and to reinforce that the Framework is not designed or intended to create additional requirements for owners and operators of critical infrastructure, who are otherwise subject to regulatory requirements.

As NIST learns from individual organizations about their experiences with the Framework—good or otherwise—NIST hopes to share that knowledge and insight with others so that they may gain confidence in using the Framework. NIST also hopes to provide specifics, for example, through appropriate "case studies," for those who are seeking more information on how to build or improve their own cybersecurity programs.

The data that is collected and reflected will be the source information for any determinations or suggestions for changes that might be needed to the Framework going forward. The Framework is envisioned as a "living document." At this point, however, there is rather widespread agreement among workshop participants that it is too soon to consider updating the Framework, and that NIST should continue efforts to promote understanding and use of the current version. This will allow industry the time to implement, for tools and service to be built and offered, as well as for the common vocabulary of the Framework to become established. In any event, any changes that might be made to the Framework will be made through the same open, transparent and inclusive process that was used in the initial creation of the Framework.

In the months ahead, NIST will focus on the challenging aspects of implementation and will consider producing guidance that will help organizations address these challenges. No modifications or new versions of the Framework are anticipated within the next year, although NIST will continue to work on areas singled out in the *Roadmap for Improving Critical Infrastructure Cybersecurity,*[3] released the same time as the Framework. NIST also will continue to explore options for future governance of the Framework, based on NIST's appreciation of the long-term benefits of the Framework becoming a private-sector maintained process in the future.

NIST will continue, and increase, its efforts to raise awareness of the Framework, including through partnerships with other organizations. NIST's efforts will be carried out in the same open and collaborative manner which was the hallmark of the Framework's development. One priority will be to develop and disseminate informa-

---

[3]   *http://www.nist.gov/cyberframework/upload/roadmap-021214.pdf*

tion and training materials that advance use of the Framework, such as actual or exemplary illustrations of how organizations of varying sizes, types, and cybersecurity capabilities can practically employ the Framework to make themselves more secure.

National Initiative for Cybersecurity Education

I would like to provide you now with an update on NIST's work to support building a capable cybersecurity workforce—a workforce that is agile and can adapt to meet the national need to design, develop, implement, maintain and continuously improve cybersecurity, consistent with the relevant provisions of the Cybersecurity Enhancement Act of 2014.

In 2010, the National Initiative for Cybersecurity Education (NICE) was established to enhance the overall cybersecurity posture of the United States by accelerating the availability of educational, training, and workforce development resources designed to improve the cybersecurity behavior, skills, and knowledge of every segment of the population. As the lead agency for this initiative, NIST works with more than 20 Federal departments and agencies, as well as with industry and academia, to raise national awareness about risks in cyberspace, broaden the pool of individuals prepared to enter the cybersecurity profession, and cultivate a globally competitive cybersecurity workforce.

NICE has also aligned with the President's Job-Driven Training Initiative to increase the number of individuals who complete high-quality cybersecurity training and education programs and attain the skills most needed to provide a pipeline of skilled workers for industry and government.

Additional Research Areas

NIST performs research and development in related technologies, such as the usability of systems including electronic health records, voting machines, biometrics and software interfaces. NIST is performing basic research on the mathematical foundations needed to determine the security of information systems. In the areas of digital forensics, NIST is enabling improvements in forensic analysis through the National Software Reference Library and computer forensics tool testing. Software assurance metrics, tools, and evaluations developed at NIST are being implemented by industry to help strengthen software against hackers. NIST responds to government and market requirements for biometric standards by collaborating with other Federal agencies, academia, and industry partners to develop and implement biometrics evaluations, enable usability, and develop standards (fingerprint, face, iris, voice/speaker, and multimodal biometrics). NIST plays a central role in defining and advancing standards, and collaborating with customers and stakeholders to identify and reach consensus on cloud computing standards.

Conclusion

NIST recognizes that it has been entrusted with an essential role in helping industry, consumers and government to manage cybersecurity risks.

NIST is extremely committed to fulfilling that role; it is committed to improving on existing cybersecurity technical solutions, standards, guidelines, and best practices, through robust collaborations with our Federal Government partners, private sector collaborators, and international colleagues; and NIST is committed to helping to ensure that government needs stay aligned with, and are informed by, the needs of American industry.

But let us be clear, and here I am not telling this Committee anything it does not know well: even with the body of work that is now behind us, there is still much to do. NIST will continue a sustained dialogue between government and the private sector to ensure it can be responsive to ever-evolving cybersecurity challenges, and in this NIST has appreciated the support of the Committee.

Thank you for the opportunity to testify today on NIST's work in cybersecurity. I would be happy to answer any questions you may have.

10

CHARLES H. ROMINE

Charles Romine is Director of the Information Technology Laboratory (ITL). ITL, one of seven research Laboratories within the National Institute of Standards and Technology (NIST), has an annual budget of $150 million, more than 350 employees, and about 160 guest researchers from industry, universities, and foreign laboratories. Dr. Romine oversees a research program designed to promote U.S. innovation and industrial competitiveness by developing and disseminating standards, measurements, and testing for interoperability, security, usability, and reliability of information systems, including cybersecurity standards and guidelines for Federal agencies and U.S. industry, supporting these and measurement science at NIST through fundamental and applied research in computer science, mathematics, and statistics. Through its efforts, ITL supports NIST's mission, to promote U.S. innovation and industrial competitiveness by advancing measurement science, standards, and technology in ways that enhance economic security and improve our quality of life. Within NIST's traditional role as the overseer of the National Measurement System, ITL is conducting research addressing measurement challenges in information technology as well as issues of information and software quality, integrity, and usability. ITL is also charged with leading the Nation in using existing and emerging IT to help meet national priorities, including developing cybersecurity standards, guidelines, and associated methods and techniques, cloud computing, electronic voting, smart grid, homeland security applications, and health information technology.

Education

Ph.D. in Applied Mathematics from the University of Virginia

B.A. in Mathematics from the University of Virginia

The CHAIRMAN. Thank you, Dr. Romine.
Ms. Beauchesne?

STATEMENT OF ANN M. BEAUCHESNE, VICE PRESIDENT, NATIONAL SECURITY AND EMERGENCY PREPAREDNESS, U.S. CHAMBER OF COMMERCE

Ms. BEAUCHESNE. Thank you. Good morning, Chairman Thune, Ranking Member Nelson, and members of the Committee. My name is Ann Beauchesne. I am the Vice President of the U.S. Chamber's National Security and Emergency Preparedness Department. On behalf of the Chamber, I welcome the opportunity to testify before the Senate Commerce Committee regarding the business community's experience with NIST's Framework for Improving Critical Infrastructure Cybersecurity.

I want to thank the Committee for holding today's hearing. Recent cyber incidents underscore the need to keep building toward a more secure and resilient cyber future at home and globally.

The good news is that addressing sophisticated cyber threats against American businesses has gone from an IT issue to a top priority for company executives and boards of directors. My statement will focus on the successful rollout of the Framework and the positive collaboration that many businesses and government entities have developed over the past several months.

The Chamber's promotion of the Framework through our Cybersecurity Campaign, as well as the urgent need for cybersecurity information sharing legislation. It is encouraging to see that the administration has put forward its own views on cybersecurity information sharing legislation as well. Legislation is needed to help businesses improve their awareness of cyber threats, as well as to enhance their protection and response capabilities.

The Chamber believes that the development and rollout of the Framework has been a success. We view the Framework as one of the best examples of a public-private partnership in action. From conception to release, the Chamber, trade associations, and companies of all sizes and sectors collaborated closely with the administration, NIST, and the Department of Homeland Security in developing the Framework. Much of industry's favorable reaction is owed in large measure to NIST. They have treated the business community as a genuine partner and tackled a tough assignment in ways that ought to serve as a model for other agencies.

Last spring, the administration sent the business community a powerful message, saying that the Framework should remain collaborative, voluntary, and innovative over the long term, in a word, ''non-regulatory.'' Businesses need flexible solutions to respond to the rapidly changing threat environment. As threats continue to evolve, businesses must be able to adapt accordingly.

I appreciate the comments of Silver Star Communications' Jeff England who notes in his written testimony that a regulatory approach to cybersecurity distracts policymakers' attention from the root problem, that is, attacks coming from organized criminals and state-sponsored groups.

Since the Framework's release last February, industry has demonstrated its commitment to using it. Critical infrastructure are keenly aware and supportive of the Framework.

In my written testimony, I have outlined how numerous associations and trade groups are creating tools and resources for their members and holding events around the country to promote cybersecurity awareness and education of the Framework. Going forward, we urge policymakers to commit even greater resources over the next several years to grow awareness of the Framework and risk-based tools for cybersecurity.

The Chamber has launched its own cybersecurity campaign under the banner of Improving Today, Protecting Tomorrow. Last year, we organized roundtable events with State and local chambers in Chicago, Austin, Everett, and Phoenix in the run-up to our third annual cybersecurity summit in October. Each roundtable featured cybersecurity principles from the White House, DHS, NIST, as well as local FBI and Secret Service officials. At these roundtables, the Chamber and our Federal partners have urged businesses of all sizes and sectors to adopt fundamental security practices to reduce network and system weaknesses. The Chamber is planning to hold more cybersecurity roundtables this year with our Federal partners, as well as our fourth annual cybersecurity summit on October 6.

The Framework is a good start, but more work is needed to push back against skilled attackers. No single tool or approach can prevent advanced and persistent threats or state-sponsored cyber attacks. Most small and mid-sized businesses tend to lack the money and personnel to beat back highly advanced and nefarious actors.

Despite the Chamber's strong support for the Framework, the effort will be incomplete without getting information sharing legislation done. While the Chamber recognizes that the Commerce Committee does not have jurisdiction over cybersecurity information sharing legislation, we continue to push Congress to pass a bill that includes robust safeguards such as liability, regulatory, FOIA, and antitrust protections for businesses that voluntarily exchange threat data with their peers and with the Government.

Last week, 35 associations, including the Chamber, sent the Senate a letter urging lawmakers to quickly pass a cyber information sharing bill.

The Senate Intelligence Committee passed a smart and workable bill last year which earned broad bipartisan support.

Cyber attacks aimed at U.S. businesses and government entities are being launched from various sources, including sophisticated hackers, organized crime, and state-sponsored groups. Congressional action on information sharing cannot come quickly enough.

Again, I want to thank you for inviting me to be here. The Chamber looks forward to working with you and your staff, and I would be happy to answer any questions.

[The prepared statement of Ms. Beauchesne follows:]

PREPARED STATEMENT OF ANN M. BEAUCHESNE, VICE PRESIDENT, NATIONAL SECURITY AND EMERGENCY PREPAREDNESS, U.S. CHAMBER OF COMMERCE

Good morning, Chairman Thune, Ranking Member Nelson, and other distinguished members of the Committee. My name is Ann Beauchesne, and I serve as vice president of the U.S. Chamber's National Security and Emergency Preparedness Department. On behalf of the Chamber, I welcome the opportunity to testify before the Senate Commerce committee regarding the business community's experience with the National Institute of Standards and Technology's (NIST's) *Framework for Improving Critical Infrastructure Cybersecurity* (the framework).[1]

The National Security and Emergency Preparedness Department was established in 2003 to develop and implement the Chamber's homeland and national security policies. The department works through the National Security Task Force, a policy committee composed of roughly 200 Chamber members representing practically every sector of the American economy. The task force's Cybersecurity Working Group identifies current and emerging issues, crafts policies and positions, and provides analysis and direct advocacy to government and business leaders.

The need to address increasingly sophisticated threats against U.S. and global businesses has gone from an IT issue to a top priority for the C-suite and the boardroom. Chamber President and CEO Thomas J. Donohue recently said, "In an interconnected world, economic security and national security are linked. To maintain a strong and resilient economy, we must protect against the threat of cyberattacks."

My statement focuses on the successful rollout of the framework and the positive collaboration that many businesses and government entities have developed over the past several months, including our new cybersecurity campaign—*Improving Today, Protecting Tomorrow*™. I am also going to highlight policy issues—information-sharing legislation being the top legislative priority—that lawmakers and the administration need to diligently address. The information-sharing discussion puts too little emphasis on improving government-to-business sharing. The Chamber wants to expand government-to-business information sharing, which is progressing but needs improvement.[2]

The framework is a good start, but more work is needed to push back against skilled attackers. Most small and midsize businesses (SMBs) tend to lack the money and personnel to beat back highly advanced and nefarious actors, such as organized criminal gangs and groups carrying out state-sponsored attacks. No single strategy can prevent advanced and persistent threats—popularly known as APTs in cybersecurity jargon—from breaching an organization's cyber defenses.

Policymakers have not sufficiently acknowledged this expensive, practical reality. American companies should not be expected to shoulder the substantial costs of cyberattacks emanating from well-resourced bad actors such as criminal syndicates or nation-states—costs typically absorbed by national governments. Nation-states or their proxies and other sophisticated actors are apparently hacking businesses with impunity—and that has got to stop.

In addition to having policymakers acknowledge cost concerns, the Chamber would welcome working with the administration and Congress on establishing an intelligent and forceful deterrence strategy, which the United States currently lacks. U.S. policymakers need to focus on pushing back against illicit actors and not on blaming the victims of cybersecurity incidents.[3]

The Framework Is an Excellent Example of an Effective Public-Private Partnership; Critical Infrastructure Awareness of the Framework Is Strong, and Sector Activities Are Robust and Maturing

The Chamber believes that the *framework—which was released last February—* has been a success. The framework represents one of the best examples of public-private partnerships in action. NIST and stakeholders in the public and private sectors should have a great sense of accomplishment. The Chamber, sector-based coordinating councils and associations, companies, and other entities collaborated closely with NIST in developing the framework since the first workshop was held in April 2013.

Critical infrastructure sectors are keenly aware of and supportive of the framework. The Chamber understands that critical infrastructures at "greatest risk" have been identified and engaged by administration officials under the terms of the cyber executive order (EO).[4] Government officials ought to ensure that all resources, par-

---

[1] See *www.nist.gov/cyberframework.*

[2] The Chamber submitted in October 2014 similar comments to National Institute of Standards and Technology (NIST) related to businesses' awareness and use of the framework. See *http://csrc.nist.gov/cyberframework/rfi\comments\10\2014.html.*

[3] The Chamber submitted comments to the Department of Homeland Security (DHS) on cybersecurity solutions for small and midsize businesses (SMBs) in April 2014.

[4] Executive Order (EO) 13636, *Improving Critical Infrastructure Cybersecurity,* is available at *www.gpo.gov/fdsys/pkg/FR-2013-02-19/pdf/2013-03915.pdf.*

ticularly the latest cyber threat indicators, are available to these enterprises to counter increasing and advanced threats.

Further, important elements of U.S. industry are aware of the framework and are using it or similar risk management tools. Indeed, the Chamber welcomed an assessment from Michael Daniel, White House special assistant to the president and cybersecurity coordinator, who remarked on September 23, 2014, at the Chamber's third cyber roundtable in Everett, Washington, that industry's response to the framework has been "phenomenal."

A second White House official, Ari Schwartz, senior director for cybersecurity, noted on October 1, 2014, that business support for the framework has "exceeded expectations." Such recognition is constructive and helps keep the private sector engaged in using the framework and promoting it with business partners.[5]

Much of industry's favorable reaction is owed in large measure to NIST, which tackled the framework's development in ways that ought to serve as a model for other agencies and departments. In May 2014, the administration sent the business community a powerful message, saying that the framework *should* remain collaborative, voluntary, and innovative over the long term.[6] Interestingly, public focus on the framework has created visibility into industry's long-standing efforts to address cyber risks and threats—constant, dedicated, and (mostly) silent efforts that preceded the creation of the framework.[7]

Most notable, since the framework's release, industry has demonstrated its commitment to using it. Many associations are creating resources for their members and holding events across the country and taking other initiatives to promote cybersecurity education and awareness of the framework. Some examples are listed here. Associations are planning and exploring additional activities as well.

- The Alliance of Automobile Manufacturers and the Association of Global Automakers have initiated a process to establish an automobile industry sector information-sharing and analysis center (Auto-ISAC) to voluntarily collect and share information about existing or potential threats to the cybersecurity of motor vehicle electronics and in-vehicle networks.
- The American Chemistry Council (ACC) is developing sector-specific guidance based on the NIST cyber framework to further enhance and implement the council's Responsible Care® Security Code. ACC's Chemical Information Technology Center (ChemITC) is also piloting an ISAC for the chemical sector.
- The American Gas Association (AGA) has hosted a series of webinars on control system cybersecurity, is collaborating with small utilities to develop robust cybersecurity programs, and is working with companies to review and enhance their cybersecurity posture using the Oil and Natural Gas Subsector Cybersecurity Capability Maturity Model (ONG–C2M2) from the Department of Energy (DOE). Among other activities, AGA has stood up the Downstream Natural Gas Information and Analysis Center (DNG–ISAC), an ISAC designed to help support the information-sharing interests of downstream natural gas utilities.
- The American Hotel & Lodging Association (AH&LA) has conducted a series of widely attended cyber and data security webinars to assist small, medium, and large hotel and lodging businesses with implementing key information security measures and risk assessments.
- The American Water Works Association (AWWA) has created cybersecurity *guidance and a use-case tool* to aid water and wastewater utilities' implementation of the framework. The guidance is cross-referenced to the framework. This tool is serving as implementation guidance for the framework in the water and wastewater systems sector.

---

[5] See "At eight-month mark, industry praises framework and eyes next steps," *Inside Cybersecurity,* October 6, 2014, *http://insidecybersecurity.com/Cyber-Daily-News/Daily-News/at-eight-month-mark-industry-praises-framework-and-eyes-next-steps/menu-id-1075.html.*

[6] The Chamber agrees with Michael Daniel's May 22 blog, *Assessing Cybersecurity Regulations,* at *www.whitehouse.gov/blog/2014/05/22/assessing-cybersecurity-regulations.* The blog says that business and government "must build equally agile and responsive capabilities not bound by outdated and inflexible rules and procedures." The Chamber and industry partners especially urge independent agencies and Congress to adhere to the dynamic approach advocated by the administration and that is embodied in the nonregulatory, public-private framework. See June 11, 2014 letter, available at *www.uschamber.com/sites/default/files/documents/files/11June14GroupLetterT-YReplytoDanielCyberBlog\Final\0.pdf.*

[7] The online publication *Inside Cybersecurity* provides an excellent catalog of industry initiatives to implement data-and network-security best practices. See *http://insidecyber security.com/Sectors/menu-id-1149.html.*

- Members of the Communications Sector Coordinating Council (CSCC)—*made up* of broadcasting, cable, wireline, wireless, and satellite segments—have participated in multiple NIST, Department of Homeland Security (DHS), and industry association-sponsored programs, webinars, and panels. The sector is completing a year-long effort within the Federal Communication Commission's (FCC's) Communications Security Reliability and Interoperability Council (*CSRIC*) that involves more than 100 professionals who have worked to adapt the NIST framework to the sector segments and provide guidance to the industry.

- The Electricity Subsector Coordinating Council has worked with DOE to develop sector-specific guidance for using the framework. The guidance leverages existing subsector-specific approaches to cybersecurity, including DOE's *Electricity Subsector Cybersecurity Risk Management Process* **Guideline,** the *Electricity Subsector Cybersecurity Capability Maturity* **Model,** NIST's **Guidelines for Smart Grid Cyber Security,** and the North American Electric Reliability Corporation's (NERC) Critical Infrastructure Protection Cybersecurity *Standards.*

- The mutual fund industry, represented by the Investment Company Institute (ICI), has added to its committee roster a Chief Information Security Officer Advisory Committee. The committee's mission is to collaborate on cybersecurity issues and information sharing in the financial services industry and provide a cyber threat protection resource for ICI members.

- The Information Technology Industry Council (ITI) visited Korea and Japan in May 2014 and shared with these countries' governments and business leaders the benefits of a public-private partnership-based approach to developing globally workable cybersecurity policies. ITI highlighted the framework as an example of an effective policy developed in this manner, reflecting global standards and industry-driven practices. ITI principals also spoke at a U.S.-European Union (EU) workshop in Brussels in November 2014, comparing U.S. and EU policy approaches to cybersecurity and highlighting the positive attributes of the framework and its development.

- The National Association of Manufacturers (NAM) has spearheaded the D.A.T.A. (Driving the Agenda for Technology Advancement) Policy Center, providing manufacturers with a forum to understand the latest cybersecurity policy trends, threats, and best practices. The D.A.T.A. Center focuses on working with small and medium-size manufacturers to help them secure their assets.

- Through the American Petroleum Institute (API), the oil and natural gas sector has worked with DOE to complete the Oil and Natural Gas Subsector Cybersecurity Capability Maturity Model (ONG–C2M2). The oil and natural gas sector in 2014 established a new Oil and Natural Gas Information Sharing and Analysis Center (*ONG–ISAC*) to provide shared intelligence on cyber incidents, threats, vulnerabilities, and responses throughout the industry.

- The Retail Industry Leaders Association (RILA), in partnership with the National Retail Federation (NRF), has created the Retail Cyber Intelligence Sharing Center (R–CISC), featuring information sharing, research, and education and training. This ISAC enables retailers to share threat data among themselves and to receive threat information from government and law enforcement partners.

- The U.S. Chamber of Commerce has launched its national roundtable series, *Improving Today, Protecting Tomorrow* ™, recommending that businesses of all sizes and sectors adopt fundamental Internet security practices.

The Chamber's New Cybersecurity Campaign Enters Its Second Year; Policymakers Need to Focus on Passing Information-Sharing Legislation and Deterring Foreign Attackers

The NIST framework is designed to help s start a cybersecurity program or improve an existing one. The framework puts cybersecurity into a common language for organizations to better understand their cybersecurity posture, set goals for cybersecurity improvements, monitor their progress, and foster communications with internal and external stakeholders.

Looking ahead to 2015, the Chamber's cybersecurity campaign intends to focus on several areas, including the following:

- *Organizing roundtables with local chambers and growing market solutions.* The Chamber is planning more cyber roundtables in 2015. Last year, the Chamber organized roundtable events with state and local chambers in Chicago, Illinois (May 22); Austin, Texas (July 10); Everett, Washington (September 23); and

Phoenix, Arizona (October 8) prior to the Chamber's Third Annual Cybersecurity Summit on October 28.

Leading member sponsors of the campaign were American Express, Dell, and Splunk. Other sponsors were the American Gas Association, Boeing, the Edison Electric Institute, Exelon, HID Global, Microsoft, Oracle, and Pepco Holdings, Inc., and *The Wall Street Journal.*

Each roundtable featured cybersecurity principals from the White House, DHS, NIST, and local FBI and U.S. Secret Service officials. The Chamber and our partners urged businesses to adopt fundamental Internet security practices to reduce network and system weaknesses and make the price of successful hacking increasingly steep. The Chamber also urged businesses to improve their cyber risk management processes. All businesses should understand common online threats that can lead them to become victims of cybercrime. Using the framework and similar risk management tools, such as the Chamber's *Internet Security Essentials for Business 2.0* guidebook,[8] is ultimately about making your business more secure and resilient. The Chamber encouraged businesses to report cyber incidents. Perfect online security is unattainable, even for large businesses. Innovative solutions are regularly being brought to market because cyber threats are always changing. Businesses should report cyber incidents and online crime to their FBI or U.S. Secret Service field offices.

- *Increasing public awareness of the framework.* The Chamber urges policymakers to commit greater resources over the next several years to growing awareness of the framework and risk-based solutions through a national education campaign. A broad-based campaign involving federal, state, and local governments and multiple sectors of the U.S. economy would spur greater awareness of cyber threats and aggregate demand for market-driven cyber solutions.

  The Chamber believes that government—particularly independent agencies— should devote their limited time and resources to assisting resource-strapped enterprises, not trying to flex their existing regulatory authority. After all, while businesses are working to detect, prevent, and mitigate cyberattacks originating from sophisticated criminal syndicates or foreign powers, they shouldn't have to worry about regulatory or legal sanctions.

- *Improving information-sharing is job No. 1.* The framework would be incomplete without enacting information-sharing legislation that removes legal and regulatory penalties to quickly exchange data about threats to U.S. companies.

  » *Passing legislation this year.* Last week, 35 associations, including the Chamber, strongly urged the Senate to quickly pass a cybersecurity information-sharing bill.[9] The Senate Intelligence committee passed a smart and workable bill in July 2014, which earned broad bipartisan support. Recent cyber incidents underscore the need for legislation to help businesses improve their awareness of cyber threats and enhance their protection and response capabilities.

    Above all, the Chamber urges Congress to send a bill to the president that gives businesses legal certainty that they have safe harbor against frivolous lawsuits when voluntarily sharing and receiving threat indicators and countermeasures in real time and taking actions to mitigate cyberattacks. The legislation also needs to offer protections related to public disclosure, regulatory, and antitrust matters in order to increase the timely exchange of information among public and private entities.

    The Chamber also believes that legislation needs to safeguard privacy and civil liberties and establish appropriate roles for civilian and intelligence agencies. The cybersecurity measure approved in July 2014 by the Senate Intelligence committee reflected practical compromises among many stakeholders on these issues.

    Cyberattacks aimed at U.S. businesses and government entities are being launched from various sources, including sophisticated hackers, organized crime, and state-sponsored groups. These attacks are advancing in scope and complexity. Congressional action cannot come quickly enough.

  » *Helping SMBs mitigate attacks.* The cybersecurity EO elevates the importance of bidirectional information sharing and calls for expanding the public-private

---

[8] The booklet is available free for downloading at *www.uschamber.com/issue-brief/internet-security-essentials-business-20.*

[9] The coalition letter is available at *www.uschamber.com/sites/default/files/150127\multi-association\cyber\info-sharing\legislation\senate.pdf.*

Enhanced Cybersecurity Services (ECS) program to critical infrastructure. The administration should consider developing an ECS program that is affordable to SMBs. On the one hand, some businesses would be well equipped internally or in partnership with third-party providers to make use of cyber threat information. On the other hand, the Chamber believes that, depending on their size and abilities, most SMBs would need significant guidance and perhaps additional assistance with incorporating threat information and risk management strategies into their organizations.

- *Engaging law enforcement.* The Chamber plans to continue its close contact with the FBI and the U.S. Secret Service to build trusted public-private relationships, which are essential to confirming a crime and beginning criminal investigations. We are encouraging businesses to partner with law enforcement before, during, and after a cyber incident. FBI and U.S. Secret Service officials have participated in each of the Chamber's roundtables.

- *Harmonizing cybersecurity regulations.* Information-security requirements should not be cumulative. The Chamber believes it is valuable that agencies and departments are urged under the EO to report to the Office of Management and Budget any critical infrastructure subject to ''ineffective, conflicting, or excessively burdensome cybersecurity requirements.'' We urge the administration and Congress to prioritize eliminating burdensome regulations on businesses. One solution could entail giving businesses credit for information security regimes that exist in their respective sectors that they have adopted.[10] It is positive that Michael Daniel, the administration's lead cyber official, has made harmonizing existing cyber regulations with the framework a priority.

- *Raising adversaries' costs through deterrence.* The Chamber is reviewing actions that businesses and government can take to deter nefarious actors that threaten to empty bank accounts, steal trade secrets, or damage vital infrastructures. While we have not formally endorsed the report, the U.S. Department of State's International Security Advisory Board (ISAB) issued in July draft recommendations regarding cooperation and deterrence in cyberspace.

  The ISAB's recommendations—including cooperating on crime as a first step, exploring global consensus on the rules of the road, enhancing governments' situational awareness through information sharing, combating IP theft, expanding education and capacity building, promoting attribution and prosecution, and leading by example—are sensible and worthy of further review by cybersecurity stakeholders.[11]

  The Chamber believes that the United States needs to coherently shift the costs associated with cyberattacks in ways that are legal, swift, and proportionate relative to the risks and threats. Policymakers need to help the law enforcement community, which is a key asset to the business community but numerically overmatched compared with illicit hackers.[12]

- *Making incentives work.* In an April 2013 letter to NIST regarding businesses' use of the framework and the role of incentives, the Chamber provides its views on extending liability protections related to information-sharing legislation (see p. 6 of this statement), extending a safe harbor related to using the framework, extending SAFETY Act applicability to the framework, eliminating cybersecurity regulations, leveraging Federal procurement, and making the research and development (R&D) tax credit permanent.[13]

---

[10] The business community already complies with multiple information security rules. Among the regulatory requirements impacting businesses of all sizes are the Chemical Facilities Anti-Terrorism Standards (CFATS), the Federal Energy Regulatory Commission-North American Reliability Corporation Critical Information Protection (FERC–NERC CIP) standards, the Gramm-Leach-Bliley Act (GLBA), the Health Insurance Portability and Accountability Act (HIPAA), and the Sarbanes-Oxley (SO_X) Act. The Securities and Exchange Commission (SEC) issued guidance in October 2011 outlining how and when companies should report hacking incidents and cybersecurity risks. Corporations also comply with many non-U.S. requirements, which add to the regulatory mix.

[11] The ISAB report is available at *www.state.gov/documents/organization/229235.pdf.*

[12] The Chamber argues for a clear cyber deterrence strategy in its December 2013 letter to NIST on the framework. See *http://csrc.nist.gov/cyberframework/framework\comments/2013 1213\ann\beauchesne\uschamber.pdf.*

[13] The letter is available at *www.ntia.doc.gov/files/ntia/29apr13\chamber\comments.pdf.*

The Chamber appreciates that the administration is assessing a mix of incentives that could induce businesses to use the framework.[14] However, in the Chamber's view, it is imperative that the administration, independent agencies, and lawmakers extend to companies the assurance that the cybersecurity framework and any actions taken in relation to it remain collaborative, flexible, and innovative over the long term. The Chamber believes that the presence of these qualities, or the lack thereof, would be a key determinant to use of the framework by U.S. critical infrastructure as well as businesses generally.

Roadmap for the Future of the Cybersecurity Framework

In February 2014, NIST released a *Roadmap* to accompany the framework. The *Roadmap* outlines further areas for possible "development, alignment, and collaboration."[15] The Chamber noted in an October 2014 letter to NIST some key areas that we see as needing more attention. The Chamber would highlight for the Committee the importance of aligning international cybersecurity regimes with the framework.

Many Chamber members operate globally. We appreciate that NIST has been actively meeting with foreign governments to urge them to embrace the framework. Like NIST, the Chamber believes that efforts to improve the cybersecurity of the public and private sectors should reflect the borderless and interconnected nature of our digital environment.

Standards, guidance, and best practices relevant to cybersecurity are typically industry driven and adopted on a voluntary basis; they are most effective when developed and recognized globally. Such an approach would avoid burdening multinational enterprises with the requirements of multiple, and often conflicting, jurisdictions.[16] The administration should organize opportunities for stakeholders to participate in multinational discussions. The Chamber encourages the Federal Government to work with international partners and believes that these discussions should be stakeholder driven and occur on a routine basis.

The Public and Private Sectors Need to Increase the Framework's Success by Improving Collaboration and Eliminating Barriers to Smart and Efficient Cybersecurity

NIST and multiple stakeholders produced a smart framework that participants can take pride in. But more work lies ahead. The Chamber looks forward to working with policymakers to ensure that preexisting regulations are harmonized with the collaborative and voluntary nature of the framework. Businesses also seek the enactment of information-sharing legislation to achieve timely and actionable situational awareness to improve detection, mitigation, and response capabilities.

The Chamber is committed to protecting America's business community and enhancing the Nation's resilience against an array of physical and cyber threats. Government and business entities need to continue leveraging the framework to strengthen collective resilience and security and make ongoing improvements. We look forward to working with Congress and the administration to build on the progress that we—industry and government—have made together.

The CHAIRMAN. Thank you, Ms. Beauchesne.
Mr. Smocer?

STATEMENT OF PAUL N. SMOCER, PRESIDENT OF BITS, FINANCIAL SERVICES ROUNDTABLE

Mr. SMOCER. Thank you, Mr. Chairman. Last year, with this committee's stewardship, Congress passed the Cybersecurity Enhancement Act of 2014. The Act's focus on an open, voluntary cybersecurity framework development process and its emphasis on cybersecurity R&D, career development, awareness, and education improve the information security of our country's cyber ecosystem.

---

[14] See *www.whitehouse.gov/blog/2013/08/06/incentives-support-adoption-cybersecurity-framework*.

[15] The *Roadmap* is available at *www.nist.gov/cyberframework/upload/roadmap-021214.pdf*.

[16] The Chamber sent a letter in September 2013 to Dr. Andreas Schwab, member of the European Parliament's Internal Market and Consumer Protection Committee, recommending amendments to the proposed European Union (EU) cybersecurity directive. The Chamber argues that cybersecurity and resilience are best achieved when organizations follow voluntary global standards and industry-driven practices.

The act's passage signaled Congress' commitment to cultivate the public-private partnership so essential to our Nation's security.

Now we are witnessing a new era of attacks by organized crime syndicates and nation states. These attacks threaten the availability of services and threaten individual's privacy and even the accuracy of their information through data manipulation or destruction. This growing threat endangers all institutions in our sector and companies in other sectors.

The financial sector has historically made huge investments in security and in driving collaboration across industries and with government. Our institutions invest because they recognize their customers trust them, but individual institution's investments can only do so much as the cyber ecosystem extends beyond any one company. Companies connect with sectors, across sectors, and with the government. The reliance on each other gives us all a critical role in the cyber landscape and requires coordinated action for the most effective response.

Recognizing the necessity for collaboration, our sector has facilitated a series of collaborative activities, as I note in my written testimony, including a significant effort around the development of the NIST Cybersecurity Framework. Let me spend some time on the Framework.

As a leader in cybersecurity, our sector wanted to be engaged in the Framework's development. From the onset, BITS, as an organization and as a representative for the Financial Sector Coordinating Council, participated with NIST. We took part in all the workshops, providing our diverse membership's perspectives. We appreciated the opportunity to be a major contributor. We wanted to ensure the Framework addressed our sector's attributes, and we wanted to understand how it would harmonize with our existing requirements. We applaud the NIST development engaged so many other sectors. NIST's inclusive approach is reflected in today's broad embrace of the Framework.

Our members use the Framework to communicate ideas and achieve buy-in for various cybersecurity initiatives. They use it to communicate expectations and requirements to their vendors.

Given its age, the Framework's uses are still evolving. One evolution we see is its use as a baseline for cyber insurance underwriting. A critical next step in the Framework's evolution will involve ways independent regulators align their expectations with it. We are concerned with a lack of a uniform approach across all regulators. Last week, BITS provided input to the Cybersecurity Forum for Independent and executive branch Regulators urging harmonization of regulatory requirements. Some agencies have charted divergent paths not aligning with the Framework or its collaborative process. Consequently, companies will need to devote time to manage a patchwork of incompatible agency requirements and invest funding in potentially duplicative efforts. This strains already taxed security resources. We ask this committee as part of its oversight to encourage agencies to focus on coordination and harmonization.

The NIST Cybersecurity Framework is very helpful in mitigating cyber risk, but we need to do more to end the cyber threat and Congress can help. We strongly believe passing effective cyber threat information sharing legislation would bolster the Framework. Our sector has worked with prior Congresses toward the development of a bipartisan bill. We hope in this Congress we witness the enactment of legislation that incentivizes the real-time sharing of cyber threat indicators amongst companies within and between sectors and with the Government and provides a targeted level of liability and disclosure protection, offers a good faith defense for sharing, and includes appropriate levels of privacy and civil liberties protections.

Protecting consumers, companies, and the Nation must remain our collaborative focus. The ability to share information is at the core of our Nation's response to the current cyber threat. We are encouraged by the recent bipartisan progress and will continue to advocate for effective legislation.

In conclusion, the NIST Cybersecurity Framework benefits and strengthens the overall cybersecurity of organizations across the cyber ecosystem. It is important in combating the growing threat of cyber attacks. With that said, we can do more to encourage its voluntary adoption, particularly encouraging agencies to coordinate and harmonize their cybersecurity guidance to avoid duplicative requirements.

Thank you again for inviting me to testify on this critical issue. Chairman Thune, Ranking Member Nelson, we look forward to working closely with you and the rest of the Committee on this important issue.

[The prepared statement of Mr. Smocer follows:]

PREPARED STATEMENT OF PAUL N. SMOCER, PRESIDENT OF BITS, FINANCIAL SERVICES ROUNDTABLE

Chairman Thune, Ranking Member Nelson, Members of the Committee, thank you for this opportunity to appear before you today to address the important topic of cybersecurity and the evolution of public and private efforts to protect critical infrastructure from cyber threats.

My name is Paul Smocer, and I am the President of BITS, the technology policy division of the Financial Services Roundtable (FSR). FSR is a trade association representing the country's leading financial service companies. Our members include banking, insurance, asset management, finance, and payment companies. Cybersecurity has been a key focus area for FSR and our companies for decades. Since 1996, BITS has played an important leadership role in cybersecurity, fraud reduction, third-party vendor management, payments and emerging technologies. BITS addresses issues at the intersection of financial services, technology, and public policy.

Cyber Threat Environment

Late last year, with this Committee's stewardship, Congress passed the Cybersecurity Enhancement Act of 2014 (Public Law No: 113–274). We believe the Act's focus on supporting and facilitating an open and voluntary cybersecurity standards development process is an important step in improving the overall information security of our country's cyber ecosystem. Moreover, we applaud the Act's emphasis on cybersecurity research and development, cybersecurity career development, and cyber awareness and education. Indeed, with the passage of this Act, Congress has signaled its commitment to cultivate the public-private partnership—a partnership that is essential to our Nation's security.

Even with these improvements, more needs to be done. The current cyber threat environment is grim. Each day, cyber risk grows as attacks increase in number, pace, and complexity. We are no longer in the days wherein the threat was confined to individual hacktivists and fraudsters. We are now in an era of attacks by not only organized crime syndicates, but also nation-states. Correspondingly, the attacks have grown beyond webpage vandalism and fraud into large-scale attacks that threaten the availability of services to citizens and threaten the privacy and accuracy of their information. Our sector is increasingly concerned with these threats, particularly with the potential for attacks that could undermine the integrity of the financial system through data manipulation or destruction. This growing threat affects all institutions in our sector regardless of size or type of financial institution including large and small, banks, credit unions, insurers and investment firms. Increasingly, and as we have recently witnessed, other sectors face these same threats.

As mentioned, with each day that passes, the cyber threat against our Nation's critical infrastructure, private sector companies, and individuals' privacy intensifies. According to Symantec's 2014 "Internet Security Threat Report," the number of targeted spear-phishing campaigns in 2013 rose by 91 percent over the previous year. These campaigns are a key method used by cyber attackers to infiltrate victim's systems and gather information. In recent years, we have also witnessed serious and significant attacks from various nation-state actors and organized criminals on the Estonian, Georgian, and Ukrainian telecommunications systems;[1] European power plants;[2] a U.S. public utility;[3] the NASDAQ;[4] Target and other major retailers and their customers.[5] Moreover, a recent report reveals that of the estimated $2–3 trillion generated annually from the "internet economy," cybercrime alone extracts between 15 percent and 20 percent of that total value.[6] In response, the private sector has increased its spending on cybersecurity, with one financial services firm spending as much as $250 million a year.

The quote often attributed to Willie Sutton that he robbed banks "because that's where the money is" reminds us as to why financial institutions are often the subject of cyber-attacks. Being a focus of the attacks is certainly one reason why the financial sector has historically led the way in making huge investments in not only security infrastructure and the best-qualified people to maintain the systems, but also in driving collaboration across industries and with the government. The primary reason for these investments though is the recognition that our customers trust us to protect them—to protect their investments, their records and their information. Individual financial institutions invest in personnel, infrastructure, services, and top of the line security protocols to protect their customers and themselves and to respond to cyber-attacks. These investments protect the individual institutions and their customers, but on its own, an individual institution generally only has the ability to protect what is within its "four walls of the company". However, as we all know, companies do not exist only within those walls. We are connected within our sector, across sectors, and with the government. This reliance on each other gives all of us a unique and critical role in the cyber landscape and requires coordinated action for the most effective response. Recognizing the cyber threat environment continues to expand in complexity and frequency and that individual institution efforts alone will not be enough, executives from the financial services sector have stepped up efforts to work together.

Financial Sector Collaborations

Our sector has facilitated a series of collaborations that resulted in a number of achievements, such as:

- The development of the Financial Services Information Sharing and Analysis Center (FS–ISAC) in 1999, which has grown in membership and capabilities since then, and significantly helped the sector response to the 2012–2013 distributed denial of service attacks (DDoS) preventing wide-scale outages;
- Creation of Soltra Edge, an initiative that will help standardize and automate the flow of real-time cyber threat information;

[1] Reuters, "Ukraine: Cyberattack on communications, MPs phones blocked," *http://www.cnbc.com/id/101465198*, (March 4, 2014).

[2] Symantec Security Response, "Dragonfly: Western Energy Companies Under Sabotage Threat," *http://www.symantec.com/connect/blogs/dragonfly-western-energy-companies-under-sabotage-threat*, (June 30, 2014).

[3] ICS–CERT Monitor, "Internet Accessible Control Systems At Risk," *https://ics-cert.us-cert.gov/sites/default/files/Monitors/ICS–CERT\Monitor\%20Jan-April2014.pdf*, (January–April 2014).

[4] Michael Riley, "How Russian Hackers Stole the Nasdaq," *http://www.businessweek.com/articles/2014–07–17/how-russian-hackers-stole-the-nasdaq*, (July 17, 2014).

[5] Symantec Corporation, " Internet Security Threat Report 2014," *http://www.symantec.com/content/en/us/enterprise/other\resources/b-istr\main\report\v19\21291018.en-us.pdf*, (April 2014).

[6] Center for Strategic and International Studies, "Net Losses: Estimating the Global Cost of Cybercrime Economic impact of cybercrime II, *http://www.mcafee.com/us/resources/reports/rp-economic-impact-cybercrime2.pdf*, (June 2014).

- Collaborating with the merchant and retail community to share best practices on cybersecurity, information sharing and payments security; and
- The significant and coordinated financial services industry effort during the development of the NIST Cybersecurity Framework.

The NIST Cybersecurity Framework

Almost two years ago, President Obama issued Executive Order 13636, calling for the development of a voluntary cybersecurity framework by the National Institute of Standards and Technology (NIST). The executive order directed NIST to seek private sector input through a collaborative process. From the outset, BITS/FSR—both as an organization and as a sector representative for the Financial Services Sector Coordinating Council (FSSCC)—participated in the NIST Cybersecurity Framework's development by taking part in all six NIST-facilitated workshops, providing the perspective of our uniquely diverse membership to this important effort. We appreciated the opportunity to be one of the major contributors to NIST's hard work that almost a year ago today, resulted in NIST's release of the Framework for Improving Critical Infrastructure Cybersecurity.

The financial services sector is often credited, and rightly so, as being one of leaders in cybersecurity. That is why we wanted to be a part of the Framework's development. We wanted to ensure the eventual framework addressed our unique sector attributes, and we wanted to understand how it would harmonize our existing requirements. We recognized too that in an interconnected world, we as a sector are not an island unto ourselves. We need and rely on entities that provide us with information technology, power, telecommunications and other critical services. We applaud that NIST's process for developing the Framework engaged these other sectors during the Framework's drafting. NIST's successful approach at inclusion of so many essential parties is reflected in how broadly embraced the Framework has become across so many sectors.

With respect to the Framework, its true value is that it synthesizes a process for cyber risk management that is accessible from the boardroom to the operations floor, across not only individual enterprises but also entire sectors. It relies on international standards and is consistent with the regulatory requirements that have been in place for our sector for more than a decade. It is a ''Rosetta Stone'' in that it provides a common lexicon for categorizing and managing cyber risks across sectors and enterprises for various unifying risk management jargons and creates a common understanding around various risk management terms, methodologies, ideas and language.

As a result, we have heard from member financial institutions that in terms of internal enterprise usage, Chief Information Security Officers (CISOs) are using the Framework to communicate ideas and achieve ''buy-in'' for various cybersecurity initiatives. Externally, firms are beginning to use it to communicate expectations and requirements to vendors. That said the Framework has only been in circulation for a relatively short time. This is an important fact for this Committee to keep in mind as it reviews the Framework at its anniversary. Because it has been only one year—one budget cycle for most firms—usage from institution to institution varies. Appropriately, the number of institutions that are aware and use the Framework, and the ways in which the Framework will be used, will evolve over time. An example of how the Framework continues to permeate new industries is its progressing role in the insurance space. The potential for the Framework to act as a baseline standard for cyber-insurance underwriters shows a new level of possibility and versatility for the voluntary standards.

Regarding the Framework development process, it was a success due in large part to its transparency and because it sought to harmonize various views into a cohesive whole. Indeed, BITS/FSR continues to participate in the evolution and maturation of the Framework through NIST's ongoing activities. For example, later this month we will be participating as a sector representative at NIST's ''Cybersecurity and Consumer Protection Summit: Executive Technical Workshop on Improving Cybersecurity and Consumer Privacy'' at Stanford University.

Just last week, BITS provided input to the Cybersecurity Forum for Independent and Executive Branch Regulators, which is comprised of all the independent regulators that are looking at ways to align and harmonize with the Framework and thus increase overall effectiveness and consistency of regulatory authorities' cybersecurity efforts pertaining to critical infrastructure. BITS reviewed how financial institutions manage cybersecurity risks, comply with comprehensive regulatory requirements, and collaborate to mitigate cyber risks. We urged the regulators to focus on harmonizing regulatory requirements to reduce regulatory compliance burdens and to focus resources on mitigating cyber risk.

However, the process has not been uniform across all stakeholders. In the year since the Framework's release, some Federal and state agencies have charted similar yet divergent paths to enhancing cybersecurity that do not embrace the Framework's open and collaborative process, instead favoring agency-unique approaches that often do not align with the Framework. As a result, information security practitioners have had to devote their time to managing a patchwork of conflicting agency efforts and organizations have to invest funding in potentially duplicative efforts, which are significant drains on available resources. While some may say that is the "cost of doing business", such a statement ignores the current reality: There is already a recognized shortage of security professionals and money needing to be increasingly invested in cybersecurity limits investment in new products to serve consumers.

Thus, we would urge this Committee, as part of its oversight function, to encourage agencies to focus more on coordination and harmonization.

Financial Top Level Domains

Like the process behind the NIST Framework, the financial services industry is no stranger to voluntary processes designed to benefit the greater good. I would like to highlight two of our most recent successes: .BANK and .INSURANCE, and Soltra Edge.

As background, in 2008, the Internet Corporation for Assigned Names and Numbers (ICANN) approved its new generic Top-Level Domains Program. This program in 2013 opened the door to a land rush on new top-level domains—the top-level domains we were accustomed to such as .COM and .ORG are no longer the only suffixes available. For a time we advocated against this domain name expansion especially as it related to financial services oriented domains out of concern for customer confusion, potential for increased malicious activity and ultimately increased costs to brand holders. When it became clear our concerns would not be addressed, the Financial Services Roundtable/BITS and the American Bankers Association, along with other financial services organizations, partnered to create a new registry operator dedicated specifically to the financial services sector—fTLD Registry Services, LLC.

This newly created organization submitted community-based applications for .BANK and .INSURANCE. I say community because unlike some entrepreneurs who have entered this space with little or no concern for protecting financial institutions or their customers, fTLD is dedicated to serving and protecting the global financial services industry. This is evidenced by the more than 120 financial services domestic and international entities who directly or through others endorsed our applications on behalf of the industry.

Besides being a financial services' owned, operated and governed registry, fTLD's domains of BANK and .INSURANCE will go beyond being simply an alternative to the legacy domains of .COM and .ORG. These domains will have robust operational requirements including eligibility, verification and name selection standards as well as enhanced technical requirements including, but not limited to, Domain Name Security Extensions (DNSSEC), strong encryption standards and e-mail authentication requirements to mitigate for example phishing and spoofing activities. fTLD is also planning other innovative uses that will be announced at a later date. All of these enhanced requirements and capabilities could only happen when individual organizations voluntarily came together to work towards a better and safer Internet.

Secondly, I want to highlight Soltra Edge, a threat intelligence-sharing platform created by a joint venture between FS–ISAC and the Depository Trust and Clearing Corporation and voluntarily funded by contributions from the financial services community. Soltra Edge is a software solution that supercharges the current information-sharing model to make it more automated and collaborative so that trusted, actionable intelligence from disparate sources can be uniformly disseminated in near real time to defend more effectively against cyber threats. The software for Soltra Edge only takes a few minutes to download and install with the basic license completely free, making this solution accessible to the largest and smallest financial institutions.

While this effort started in the financial services sector, we expect the technology behind Soltra Edge to be adopted broadly by other critical sectors including healthcare, energy, transportation, retail and others.

Though Soltra Edge represents significant progress in closing the gap between threat intelligence sharing and implementing mitigating controls, a platform like this is still constrained by legal limitations on what information can be shared. Congress has an important role to play in filling this gap. The passage of effective cyber threat information sharing legislation is a critical step to enabling optimal sharing capability.

The Public-Private Partnership: How Congress Can Help

While the NIST Cybersecurity Framework is a helpful tool, it is not the silver bullet that puts an end to the cyber threat. As such, an institution could use the NIST Cybersecurity Framework fully and it could still be compromised. Thus, more is needed, and Congress can help. At a basic level, policymakers can help by recognizing that the firm that experiences the cyber-attack—be it a bank, retailer, or an entertainment firm—is a victim. Political leaders and regulators should work to destigmatize attacks and encourage companies to come forward and share threat information that could help other companies protect themselves, their employees and their customers.

Despite the success of the information-sharing model used by the financial services sector, more can be done. We believe the Framework would be bolstered by the passage of effective cyber threat information sharing legislation. Our sector has been focused on this effort for many years and has continued to work closely with key committees in both the House and Senate. The legislation should not be delayed. BITS/FSR has supported several pieces of information sharing legislation developed by both the House and Senate. Most recently BITS/FSR has supported the cyber threat information sharing legislation passed by the Senate Intelligence Committee last year, the Cybersecurity Information Sharing Act of 2014 (CISA). BITS/FSR worked closely with former Chair Chambliss, Vice Chair Feinstein and their staff to develop the bipartisan bill. In our view, that bill encompassed key components to help enhance the volume and scope of threat information sharing. Furthermore, the legislation had the support of not only the financial services sector but also a wide range of critical infrastructure sectors. Congress must enact legislation that incentivizes the sharing and receiving of cyber threat indicators amongst companies within sectors, between sectors, and with the government. BITS/FSR believes that for legislation to be truly effective it must include the following provisions:

- Facilitate real-time sharing to enable institutions and government to act quickly;
- Provide a targeted level of liability and disclosure protections for cyber threat information sharing and receiving between individual institutions, through existing sharing mechanisms such as our FS–ISAC, private to government, and government to private;
- Offer a good faith defense for the sharing of threat information and data;
- Provide protection from disclosure through the Freedom of Information Act or to prudential regulators;
- Facilitate the appropriate declassification of information by the intelligence agencies and expedites the issuance of clearances to appropriate private sector individuals; and
- Include appropriate levels of privacy and civil liberties requirements.

BITS/FSR is encouraged by recent bipartisan progress and will continue to advocate for legislation that will allow our members to share cyber threat information with each other, various business sectors, the government, and law enforcement, to protect their customers.

Conclusion

In conclusion, the NIST Cybersecurity Framework benefits and strengthens the overall cybersecurity posture of critical infrastructure organizations, including those sectors on which financial institutions rely. The Framework will continue to play an important role as we continue to combat the growing threat of cyber-attacks. With that said, more can be done to encourage adoption of this voluntary Framework. This Committee should use its oversight authorities to encourage agencies to coordinate and harmonize cybersecurity requests, examinations, and guidance. Security professionals and investment dollars are constrained. When different regulators place duplicative burdens on security, that takes away from resources that could be devoted to preventing cyber-attacks. That, in turn, does not help any company and ultimately weakens our ability to protect the Nation's critical infrastructure.

The risks associated with cyber-attacks and threats are vitally important to the private and public sectors. Protecting consumers, companies, and the Nation must remain the focus. The ability to share information is at the core for our Nation's response to the current cyber threat.

Thank you again for inviting me to testify on this critical issue. Chairman Thune and Ranking Member Nelson, we look forward to working closely with you and the rest of the Committee on this important issue.

The CHAIRMAN. Thank you, Mr. Smocer.
Mr. England?

STATEMENT OF JEFFERSON H. ENGLAND, CHIEF FINANCIAL OFFICER, SILVER STAR COMMUNICATIONS

Mr. ENGLAND. Chairman Thune, Ranking Member Nelson, members of the Committee, thank you very much for inviting me to be here and share with you some of my experiences as we have used the Cybersecurity Framework that NIST developed in our own organization.

In February 2013, when President Obama issued an Executive Order calling upon critical infrastructure industries to voluntarily take measures to improve their cybersecurity posture, I had just accepted this position as the Chief Financial Officer at Silver Star Communications. I am new to telecom. And as a risk manager in our organization, I knew that I had a responsibility to figure out ways to address, among other things, cybersecurity risk in our organization.

Shortly after that, I had an opportunity to visit with some of our friends at U.S. Telecom.

And as NIST had released their initial draft of the Framework, they had called upon industry representatives to provide some feedback regarding the initial draft copy of that Framework. We chose, as an organization, to go through and begin using it as best as we felt like we could as a way of providing some feedback. One of the items that we had passed along was this utilization of a gap analysis, which we know has been included in the final version of the Framework that was released, as you say, Chairman Thune, almost a year ago.

We found that the Framework has been extremely beneficial in our organization. Not only did it give our IT staff and managers a framework whereupon we could exercise disciplined cybersecurity improvements in our organization, but it forced within us an opportunity to communicate at all levels within our organization, at level that had not previously existed before. We found, as we have gone through and used this, that voluntary adoption is key to the success within our organization. First off, we felt like the ability to adapt the Framework to use within our organization—we are a small business. We have roughly 9,500 access lines in western Wyoming. We found that the ability to adapt and use it as best met our need is one of the great strengths of the Framework.

Ranking Member Nelson, you had mentioned the NIST Framework meeting that was taking place in February. I had an opportunity to speak at that conference. And in that meeting, I demonstrated some ways in which we had taken the Framework, as it exists, and used the information to build management tools where we could provide visibility within our organization regarding our progress and our activities on our cybersecurity practices in our organization.

We believe that due to the voluntary nature of the Framework, it allows us to build ourselves as an organization upon having a stronger, competitive advantage amongst our peers, and we have found, as we have adapted the use of the Framework internally that it has created opportunities for us to discuss cybersecurity risk with our customers and with our vendors in a way that we had not previously done. We were surprised, as we began using this. We called upon some of our larger suppliers to get some feedback. We were hoping to franchise from them and their policies to implement without organization, and we were surprised, as we did so, that a number of our vendors did not have written policies and procedures in place regarding cybersecurity practices. And so it created a dialogue between us and them, and we found that to be very beneficial.

And then we also found, as we have gone through and utilized the framework internally within our organization—just anecdotally I can tell you when I visited with our IT staff initially, they looked at the complete Framework. And it is voluminous. It is a wealth of information. But my IT staff immediately said this is going to take an additional one-and-a-half full-time resources to go through and complete this thing. And since we believed it was a voluntary adoption and not a checklist, I turned around to my IT staff and I said, look, you are looking at this all wrong. We are not adding work upon you. This Framework is designed to help shape how you do the work you are already doing. When we had that perspective internally and we could consider the facts that we were exposing our view into a number of areas regarding cybersecurity that we previously had not done, it had made some big improvements for us in our organization.

Finally, I would just like to go on record and make a case against regulation. We believe that regulation creates a minimum standards environment where a checklist approach is undesirable in this space. I have concern that whether it be in our organization or others, if it were a regulated requirement, it would be far easier for me to hand over the checklist to my IT staff and say complete this and turn in a report, and it would have bypassed all of the meaningful conversations that we have had within our organization.

We also believe that having a minimum set of standards puts perpetrators on alert as to where they should be focusing their attentions.

And finally, as we commented earlier by Ms. Beauchesne, we believe that going about it on a regulated approach alone is a misguided attempt by government. It has the opportunity to distract attention from the real perpetrators which are the criminals who are attacking our system. And we believe that through information sharing and other practices, that we can help focus Government attention on bringing justice to the perpetrators.

[The prepared statement of Mr. England follows:]

PREPARED STATEMENT OF JEFFERSON H. ENGLAND, CHIEF FINANCIAL OFFICER, SILVER STAR COMMUNICATIONS

Silver Star Communications, located in Freedom, WY, has been using the NIST Cyber Security Framework since it was originally released in draft form. Our initial intent was to review the framework and provide comment and feedback to NIST regarding its value to us as a rural telephone and Internet service provider. Our initial impressions were positive and some of our comments, including the incorporation of a gap analysis, ware included in the official released version of the framework.

We have found that the framework has created an environment that encourages discussion, both internal and external, regarding its application in our organization. But above all, the greatest benefit from the framework has been the ability to use and adapt it within our organization such that it has become a meaningful management tool for improved cybersecurity practices.

The framework helped provide us with a disciplined approach to reviewing cybersecurity practices within our organization. In the course of completing a self assessment, there were many processes and procedures identified that we had not previously considered. The focus on current state relative to desired state in the context of acceptable risk provided meaningful focus and direction to IT staff and management. Additionally, since the framework allowed for organizational specific adaptation, we developed an internal reporting mechanism that provided executive visibility into our progress on highest priorities.

The voluntary nature of the framework has been the key to success for use within our organization.

We believe cybersecurity to be a competitive advantage whereby we differentiate ourselves from our competitors and make ourselves more attractive to our suppliers and those we serve. Because of this, we are self driven toward improvement and have begun sharing our cybersecurity practice with those we serve more openly. Curious as to whether or not our suppliers have used the framework, we began asking them to share with us their cybersecurity practices. These conversations have been extremely valuable in helping us identify customers and suppliers who share similar cybersecurity risk tolerances to our own and has become an important part of our vendor selection process.

We also believe that a regulatory mandate requiring the use of the framework creates a minimum standard environment. We believe this to be problematic because minimum standards are more likely to be treated as a checklist that can be delegated without having the necessary interdepartmental conversations regarding exposure and acceptable risk tolerance. There is also risk that minimum standards would put perpetrators on alert as to where they should focus their attentions for exploitation potentially placing organizations at additional cybersecurity risk than before.

Finally, we believe that a regulated approach to cybersecurity may, at least in part, misplace government attention away from the root problem. Cyber attackers are criminals and state sponsored cyber attacks are acts of war. Government action regarding cybersecurity should place primary emphasis on tracking down and bringing cyber criminals to justice.

The CHAIRMAN. Thank you, Mr. England.
Dr. Lewis?

STATEMENT OF DR. JAMES A. LEWIS, DIRECTOR AND SENIOR FELLOW, STRATEGIC TECHNOLOGIES PROGRAM, CENTER FOR STRATEGIC AND INTERNATIONAL STUDIES

Dr. LEWIS. Thank you, Mr. Chairman, and I thank the Committee for the opportunity to testify.

Executive Order 13636, Improving Critical Infrastructure Cybersecurity, released in 2013 was a major shift in U.S. policy on cybersecurity. One of the flaws in the 2012 comprehensive Senate legislation was it tried to give a single agency the authority to regulate cyberspace. The EO, by tasking sector-specific agencies to use the Framework for better cybersecurity, is a better approach. The executive order instructed NIST to develop a Cybersecurity Framework to guide companies in securing critical infrastructure. The process is voluntary, as you have heard. This executive order is likely to be followed by another on information sharing in early 2015.

These executive actions are the building blocks for better cybersecurity. But what we want to think about is are they adequate. And the primary measurement for adequacy is are we stopping opponents from getting in. Adoption is not a good measure for success. Even if all companies adopt the Framework, it does not mean better cybersecurity. The only way to measure effectiveness is to ask if the number of successful penetrations in the outflow of data has decreased. If hackers still get in and data still flows out, the Framework needs to be further amended.

In 2013, the FBI notified 3,000 companies that they had been hacked and lost data. There may have been more. If this number declines in 2015, it says the Framework is working.

Judging from the news, however, the number of successful attacks against U.S. companies has not decreased. We do not know if this is because companies have not adopted the Framework or if they have been unable to implement it or if it is because the Framework is in itself ineffective.

For example, it appears that Sony had not implemented the NIST Framework, but even if it had, the North Koreans still would have gotten in. And North Korea is the least skilled of our likely opponents.

Implementing the NIST Framework is not easy. Many small and medium-sized companies lack the manpower, training, and resources to implement the Framework.

Cost is an important issue for companies of all sizes. Improving cybersecurity asks a business to spend money on things it will not generate a return on investment, and we do not have a mechanism for them to recoup costs.

This means that cybersecurity involves a business decision by companies about how much risk they will take and how much they are willing to spend to lower that risk. Many companies still underestimate risk, and the Framework provides a good way for them to rethink their approach to cybersecurity.

The Framework could be seen as part of an emerging national approach to cybersecurity, shaped by Government action and economic incentives. These incentives come from regulation, market risk, and civil liability. The Framework helps regulators and companies manage risk in critical infrastructure. Federal Trade Commission actions and consumer reaction will incentivize companies to better protect personal information.

The Federal Government needs to do more to discourage cyber espionage, but companies need to do better at defense. The market will penalize companies that have under-prioritized cybersecurity, and companies face the risk of civil liability because a case could be made that a company that has not implemented the NIST Framework has failed to exercise due diligence. And I think this will have a powerful shaping effect over the next couple of years.

Now, is all of this enough for better cybersecurity? Probably not. But it is a good start, and the NIST Framework is a step forward in what is going to be a long process to make this Nation more secure.

With that, I thank you and I am happy to take your questions.

[The prepared statement of Dr. Lewis follows:]

PREPARED STATEMENT OF DR. JAMES A. LEWIS, DIRECTOR AND SENIOR FELLOW, STRATEGIC TECHNOLOGIES PROGRAM, CENTER FOR STRATEGIC AND INTERNATIONAL STUDIES

I thank the Committee for the opportunity to testify on private sector experience with the National Institute of Standard's (NIST) Cybersecurity framework. The Framework provides a list of measures companies can take it improve their cybersecurity. I will discuss three issues: what we know about the Framework's adoption, how effective it is, and where it can be improved.

An initial conclusion is we lack sufficient data to say definitively whether the Framework is working or not to build a more secure cyber future. The Framework itself was released relatively recently, in February 2014. It will take more time for the Framework to be implemented, adjusted and to see if it what effect it has on cybersecurity. My comments on the Framework are best seen as preliminary until we have gained further experience and data on its implementation. On the larger issue of building a more secure cyber future, in which the NIST Framework may play a part, there is sufficient data and experience to describe the situation and to make general recommendations for improvement,

Executive Order (EO) 13636, "Improving Critical Infrastructure Cybersecurity," released in February 2013 was a major shift in U.S. policy on cybersecurity. Instead of making a single agency responsible for cybersecurity, it assigned responsibility to existing, sector-specific regulatory agencies. The EO instructed the National Institutes of Standards and Technology to develop a "Cybersecurity Framework" released in February 2014, that companies could use to guide their defensive efforts and that agencies could use to measure if the critical infrastructure companies they regulated were doing an adequate job. The process is voluntary. In addition, approximately 200 critical infrastructure companies were notified by the White House that they would be held to a higher level of scrutiny given their strategic importance. This Executive Order is likely to be followed by another executive action in early 2015 on information sharing. The executive actions and the NIST Framework are building blocks for better cybersecurity, but while they are good first steps, the U.S. remains vulnerable.

We should, if the Framework is effective in improving cybersecurity, see changes in the attacker population, with the less skilled attackers dropping out and the more skilled (or better resourced) changing attack techniques. Even if the Framework is effective now, if it is not dynamic and evolve along with the threats we face, it might not produce a lasting decrease in the rate of data exfiltration, as skilled opponents adjusts to improved defenses. This outcome is possible if the attacker seeking to exfiltrate data is an intelligence agency or foreign military who have the resources and dedication to wage a persistent campaign.

For example, and judging from public sources, it appears that Sony had not implemented most of the NIST Framework recommendations, but it is not clear that even if it had, North Korea would have been prevented from gaining access and doing damage. The defenses needed for determined State opponents like Iran and North Korea lie outside the NIST Framework.

One way to think about critical infrastructure is from the perspective of an enemy "targeteer," planning what American targets to strike with cyber attacks in order to achieve the desired military effect. For these opponents, America is a target rich environment, with thousand of potential targets, many of which are poorly defended. If the opponent wishes to make a political statement, it will look for a single poorly defended target with symbolic or political value. If the desired effect is temporary military advantage, it might strike a few dozen civilian targets—logistics systems and perhaps critical infrastructure in the areas that would support deployed U.S. forces, in Hawaii and the West Coast, for example, if the conflict was with forces under PACCOM. If the desired effect was extensive damage to the U.S. economy and military capabilities, a broad campaign with hundreds of civilian targets would need to be attacked. Fortunately, this attack scenario is very unlikely and only one or two countries have this capability.

The EO 13636 process attempted to identify some of these critical civilian targets, but in general we have no idea whether the Framework complicates opponent planning for cyber attack. The dilemma for cyber security is that, unlike other possible attacks against the U.S., we have not found an effective defensive strategy. Our military forces deter truly damaging attacks—no country willingly seeks war with the U.S.—but they did not deter North Korea from damaging Sony or Iran from attempting to damage banks. We need a blend of adequate defenses at the company level and robust Federal efforts to dissuade opponents if we are to build a secure cyber future and while the right formula has not been found, the NIST strategy could form a useful part of an effective national approach to cybersecurity.

A compliance approach to security lists actions taken; a better approach is to ask to see the results of those actions. Good data on results is unavailable, and much of the discussion of cybersecurity is strangely disconnected from fact. The primary categories for measurement are the number of companies adopting of the Framework and its effectiveness in thwarting opponents.

But adoption is not an adequate measurement for success. Even if all companies were to voluntarily implement the NIST Framework, it does not necessarily mean that there will be an improvement in cybersecurity. The measures listed by NIST are likely to improve security if implemented correctly, but to what degree there will be improvement is unknown, nor do we have any idea of how many companies have implemented the Framework recommendations, or how well they have done so. For example, if there was widespread adoption of the framework but little effect on penetration and exfiltration, it would be premature to say that the tide has turned in cyberspace. The difficulty in linking recommendation and effect strongly affects how we manage risk, and the lack of data hampers a range of initiatives, from creating a cyber insurance market to applying the NIST Framework.

The only way to accurately measure effectiveness is to ask if the number of successful penetrations and the outflow of data have decreased. If hackers still get in and data still flows out, the Framework is not working. These are result-based measures, fundamental for determining the return on investment in cybersecurity. Many things can be asserted or even measured, but they are useful only to the extent they can be correlated with effects.

Judging from the news, the number of successful computer breaches against U.S. companies and agencies has not decreased. We do not know if this is because companies have not adopted the framework, have been unable to implement it, or if it is because the Framework is ineffective. An initial estimate is that all three of these estimates are likely true, but to guide policy and legislation we need to understand whether which is the most likely cause for the absence of a visible improvement in U.S. cybersecurity.

The success rate of opponents, determined by their ability to penetrate target computer networks and to exfiltrate data from these networks, is the only true measure of the Framework's effectiveness. In 2013, press reports state that the FBI notified 3000 companies that they had been hacked—and there may have been more that we do not know about. If this number declines in 2015, it indicates that the Framework is successful.

NIST did put out a Request for Information (RFI) on the private sector's experience so far with using the agency's cybersecurity framework and in October it received more than fifty responses form companies and associations. A majority of respondents were supportive of the Framework and acknowledged its increasing adoption in various sectors. Other comments included support for the Framework's easily understood guidance, worries that small and medium size enterprises were not capable of meeting the guidelines due to costs, and confusion about the voluntary nature of the Framework. A majority of respondents called for continued support for the Framework.

A Request for Information is not the best approach to assessment, because companies that report "self-select," with only those with good stories to tell providing a response. There will be a desire to say that the Framework is working well, as this would remove the impetus for further cybersecurity measures. These are normal problems with survey data, but they could skew responses to produce an overly rosy picture. An alternative approach would be to use Commerce Department (of which NIST is a part) authorities under the Defense Production Act (DPA) to require companies to respond. Using the DPA would allow Commerce to devise an adequate sample of companies that would allow it to estimate adoption rates by sector and company size. Other agencies also can collect information for sector specific groups. There may be some resistance to conducting a survey. This resistance in itself would be a good indication of intent regarding the Framework.

There have been only few efforts, such as DHS's continuous monitoring effort and the Australian Signals Directorate work on its "Strategies to Mitigate Targeted Cyber Intrusions," to show that implementing a measure produces an observable reduction in successful attacks. These efforts allow us to say that some measures drastically reduce opponent success rate. Many of these measures are included in the Framework, along with a quantity of other.

Several issues complicate the implementation of the NIST Framework. Many small and medium sized companies lack the manpower, training and resources to fully implement the Framework. Straightforward measures, such as the ASD mitigation strategies, are appropriate from small and medium companies but may not work as well in the complicated networks of large companies. Cost is an important issue for companies of all sizes—essentially cyber security requires a business to allocate resources to purposes that will not generate a return on investment. In cybersecurity, we are asking companies to spend money on activities that do not generate a return and we have not offered any mechanisms for them to recoup this cost. Of course, a good way for companies to think about spending on cyber security is that it is like insurance, where a company spends money to reduce and manage risk.

This means that at the level of the firm, cyber security involves business decisions where companies should decide how much risk they are willing to take, what mitigation efforts (like insurance) best manage risk, and then spend accordingly on protection. Anecdotal evidence suggests that many companies still underestimate cyber security risks, but this is changing and the recent series of events, in particular the Target breach (which led to the resignation of the Chief Executive Officer and a dramatic decline in revenue), have helped to focus attention and raise awareness in company management and boards.

The Framework provides a useful focal point for company discussions of cybersecurity, and a commonly held view is that it is a good first step. Over time, it is likely that as companies implement the Framework, they will modify it and identify measures that best fit their own purposes, as they experiment with different approaches and find what works best. Each critical infrastructure sector may find that some parts of the framework are more important for their business than others and modify implementation in ways that works best for them.

The effect of the Framework on reducing cybersecurity risk might be different for critical infrastructure than for intellectual property. Survey data on penetration and exfiltration success rates will show where individual defense are inadequate and where collective action is needed, through increased international engagement in diplomacy and law enforcement cooperation to reduce cyber risks. To continue the insurance analogy, we want to take governmental actions that reduce systemic risk so that companies can spend less on ''insurance,'' *e.g.,* cybersecurity.

One of the most valuable lessons of EO 13636 is that one size does not fit all. In retrospect, one of the most serious flaws of the 2012 draft Senate legislation was its efforts to assign a single agency the authorities to regulate cyberspace. The EO, by tasking regulatory agencies to ensure that their existing regulations adequately take the Framework into account, better reflects the diversity of the economy.

What is emerging is a structure for national cybersecurity shaped by the different incentives (or lack thereof) that companies faces in making business decisions about cybersecurity. These incentives are created by are regulatory authority, business risk, and civil liability.

- Critical infrastructure: improved cybersecurity will be the result of partnerships between companies and their sector regulators. This is the area where the Framework and the Executive Order have made the most valuable contributions, since it provides a basic template against which company actions can be measured.

- Personally identifiable information: Federal Trade Commission (FTC) actions and market penalties can incentivize companies to better protect personally identifiable information, but the level of cybersecurity at major companies holding PII is has been inadequate.

- Intellectual property: there is no regulatory mechanism to penalize companies for the loss of IP, nor should there be. When a company is hacked and loses IP, a part of the responsibility is shared by the Federal Government, which needs to do more to discourage economic espionage by foreign actors, but the bulk of the responsibility is held by the company, which has made bad business decisions to under-prioritized cybersecurity. Increasingly, the market will penalize such companies, at least temporarily, and these companies face increased risk of civil liability. Shareholders and customers can now ask if a company had implemented the NIST Framework; if it had not, a case could reasonably be made that the management had failed to exercise due diligence.

From one perspective, cobbling together measures like the Framework, FTC rules, and some yet-undefined set of mechanisms for information sharing might seem like a ramshackle approach to one of the principle security problems of our time. There is some truth to this, but another perspective is that the complexity of the problem, the deeply ingrained problems with the technology, and the consequences of any cyber action for security and economics at both the global and national level, militates against any single solution that can be easily and rapidly adopted. Federal action can accelerate progress and provide structures for collective action, and from this perspective, the NIST Framework is a valuable step forward in what will be a long and uncertain process to make cyberspace more secure.

I again thank the Committee for the opportunity to Testify and would be happy to answer any questions.

The CHAIRMAN. Thank you, Dr. Lewis. You all did an exceptionally good job of staying within the 5-minute sort of not requirement, but suggestion that we have.

We will do 5-minute rounds of questions for members of the Committee who are here.

And I will start it off, Mr. England, by pointing out—I think this is your first time testifying before Congress. Is that correct?

Mr. ENGLAND. It is.

The CHAIRMAN. Welcome.

And your company, as I understand it, was formed by a bunch of ranchers in Wyoming back in the early 1900s.

Mr. ENGLAND. That is correct. Initially our telephone line was the top wire on a barbed wire fence.

The CHAIRMAN. I suspect in western Wyoming in the early 1900s, forming your own communications company was born out of necessity probably.

Mr. ENGLAND. Pretty much so.

The CHAIRMAN. Well, anyway, the point I want to make is that yours is a small rural business, and does not have the endless resources, as you mentioned, to address cybersecurity risk. And as the CFO for Silver Star, the question is, how have you been able to use the Framework in a cost effective way to guide how you protect your networks? And a follow up would be, has the common language helped you make business decisions and better communicate with your IT managers and your outside suppliers?

Mr. ENGLAND. Yes. Thank you, Chairman Thune.

To answer the first part of your question regarding the cost effectiveness, it is true that making improvements identified within the Framework costs money. That is just unavoidable. However, using the Framework within our organization did not create additional cost for us as a business. And so, as an example, when my IT staff came in and discussed with me the fact that there was a lot of information in that Framework and how are they going to dedicate time to reviewing that in addition to their regular job functions, I explained to them that they were looking about it all wrong. The Framework was a way of providing some structure to the way that they were already doing their jobs that kept it in the framework of cybersecurity improvements. So we found some very easy things that we were able to do.

As an example, one of the things that the Framework invites members to do is to consider cybersecurity risk as part of a risk management meeting. And when we looked through our whole strategic planning process internally, we knew that we were doing a risk assessment meeting to talk about any and all other risks. We had not previously considered cybersecurity risk as part of that meeting. And so in making an improvement internally, based on the suggestions provided in the Framework, we were able to add this discussion item at no cost to us, and yet it helped shape the whole way that we did the rest of our capital budgeting and everything else internally. So we found some very good benefits at minimal cost initially.

And then the second part of your question about the common language of the Framework. I think that our experience was that the Framework has five functional areas. It ranges from the beginning of identifying and responding and recover at the end. We found that on the front end, the identify, the respond and recover at the back end—these were very common understandable things for executive leaders and directors in our organization because these are things we are already trying to do as it is.

The middle sections of detect and protect were more IT focused. And so we did have to rely on our IT staff and sitting down and having conversations with them. But where the real value was is that I was able to turn to my IT staff and ask them to help me identify where our current tier assignment was, and then as an executive leader in our organization, I was able to help provide direction where our target tier, our acceptable risk levels would be.

And so this dialogue that we had between executive and IT managers regarding overall cybersecurity risk in the organization was an extreme benefit for us. And we felt that the language contained within the Framework was conducive for that type of conversation.

The CHAIRMAN. The first impulse of Government is often to regulate. I think you make a good point, Mr. England, that cybersecurity mandates can lead to minimum checklists and signal to hackers potential areas for exploitation.

Dr. Romine, you stated that NIST has reached out to regulatory agencies to reinforce the fact that the Framework is not designed or intended to create additional regulatory requirements for critical infrastructure owners and operators. And that is a principle we really worked hard to incorporate into the legislation that moved last year.

And I just want to ask you the question, why is a voluntary Framework the best approach, given the severity of the threat, and what kind of feedback have you received from other agencies?

Dr. ROMINE. Thank you, Mr. Chairman. And I appreciate the support of the Committee for all of the work that we are doing.

Our approach is to try to make sure that there is an understanding that a voluntary program does not equate to a weak program. In fact, voluntary programs for cybersecurity can be highly effective. The reason the voluntary approach I think makes the most sense is that it maintains the conversation. It maintains the engagement across sectors and provides the mechanism, as Mr. England pointed out, to incorporate the cybersecurity risk as part of the overall risk management of the enterprise whereas, as he pointed out, anything that would require adhering to regulation in this particular space—the tendency would be to push that to the IT component of the organization and just assume that that is being taken care of. And I think that is going to be far less effective.

The CHAIRMAN. Thank you.

Senator Nelson?

Senator NELSON. Mr. Romine, the voluntary program works as long as everybody is volunteering.

I look at this through two portals: data security, personal privacy; and national security.

Mr. England, I think you are right that the market will shape the requirements because if people are having their personal privacy taken away, and they go through all of that harassment, they are going to demand of the company. Now, companies naturally have a reluctance to come forward by telling that they have been invaded, and perhaps some of that loss can be taken care of by insurance, as you all have testified.

But when you get to the question of national security, the terrorist is not likely going to attack your operation, Mr. England. They are going to go for the bigger spectacular thing.

So this morning, we had six or seven people killed on the New York railroad system. All signs are that it was just a train crash into a vehicle. But how about a cyber attack on a transportation system that may shut down the railroad or cause two trains to run together? What about Target? 70 million shoppers' data taken. How about Yahoo? Passwords and user names in a cyber attack. How about EBay changing the passwords because of a cyber attack? Several banks, including J.P. Morgan, 76 million households and 7 million small businesses affected. Home Depot, 56 million accounts, $62 million to cover the cost. Sony, we already talked about, $100 million, directly a cyber attack for its intended purpose to intimidate.

So, Ms. Beauchesne, how can you say that everything is working, as you testified?

Ms. BEAUCHESNE. Thank you, sir.

Well, I would say that we do not want to have mandates on the private sector. The bad guys do not have mandates and regulations. The threat is evolving quickly. We need to have the private sector be able to evolve quickly and continue to evolve their defenses. I think the strongest incentive for the private sector is that they want to protect their information. They want to protect their customers. It is in their best interests for them to stay in business to do that. That is the incentive.

Senator NELSON. Well, as I said in the opening comments, if a terrorist comes in and with a satchel charge blows up a major electrical grid, sewer plant, water plant, that is obviously a terrorist attack. But they can do the same thing with a cyber attack where the effect even is more extensive.

Can you tell us what percent of the companies represented on your task force have actually implemented this Framework, this voluntary Framework?

Ms. BEAUCHESNE. No, sir. We have not surveyed them. I do not have an exact number for you.

But I will tell you that through our campaign that we have done around the country, all of the companies are highly interested in adopting the Framework and using the Framework. And this is not new. The Framework is a new tool but it is made up of best practices and standards and guidelines that companies have been using for several years now.

Senator NELSON. Would you submit for the Committee's consideration the percentage of that, as well as the percentage of your general membership implementing the Framework?

And, Mr. Smocer, among the publicly traded companies represented by the Business Roundtable, have any of your members identified cyber attacks as the reason for declining earnings?

Mr. SMOCER. Within the Financial Services Roundtable, to the best of my knowledge, no, not at this point.

Senator NELSON. Do they consistently report, in their SEC filings, cyber attacks?

Mr. SMOCER. With regard to the SEC filings, obviously cyber risk is one of the risks they need to consider, and if there are indications under SEC rules that that risk has importance, then yes, they are reporting it, sir.

Senator NELSON. Mr. Moran?

STATEMENT OF HON. JERRY MORAN, U.S. SENATOR FROM KANSAS

Senator MORAN [presiding]. Thank you very much.

Senator Thune indicated he was departing for a few minutes for a Finance Committee meeting, and next on the list is Mr. Peters after me.

Ms. Beauchesne, you indicated in your testimony that the NIST Framework has been a helpful tool, but then you also promoted needing to go further with information sharing. You indicated that is not the jurisdiction of this committee. But I want to explore what we can learn from NIST and the partnership that is created there to encourage that information sharing.

I probably will ask Mr. England a similar question. But how do we get the smallest businesses? What is the incentive for them to participate today, and what barriers need to be overcome to see that they do participate potentially on information sharing?

Ms. BEAUCHESNE. Thank you.

First of all, I think take a look at the Framework. It is only a year old. Right? So we are still socializing it. We are still getting people to be aware of that, and that is part of the Chamber's job, working with NIST. It has been a terrific partnership because the private sector was involved in every step of the development of the Framework. So they had a big stake in this working.

As far as getting smaller companies to adopt the Framework, the more that people are using it, the cost of adoption will go down. Right?

Senator MORAN. So the cost of participation will be——

Ms. BEAUCHESNE. A market influence, yes, sir.

Not everyone, especially the small or medium-sized businesses, can afford to go out and hire a FireEye, a Mandiant. So we want everyone to use this tool. And again, the Framework is one tool in the toolbox. It is a process. It is a great one. Everyone is talking the same language. Everyone is looking at the same kind of process.

But as you said, more needs to be done. And that is the information sharing piece, and that is the Chamber's number one cybersecurity priority this year. We really need to get that legislation done. If we are going to get to the next level so that the Federal Government shares information with the private sector, that we are seeing the threats at the same time, that we are sharing information in real time, not 6 months later when the FBI comes knocking on your door.

Senator MORAN. Do you know the description of the businesses, the kind of demographic or size, revenue, number of employees, kind of the description of the typical business that participates in the industry information sharing and analysis centers or a number of fusion centers across the country, including one in Topeka, Kansas that gets great national reviews? Is there an indication that small business is able and interested to participate?

Ms. BEAUCHESNE. I actually will defer to my colleague here on the ISAC participation. My understanding, though, is it is probably more mid-sized and large-sized companies. The smaller ones frankly do not have the staff or time that is my understanding.

Mr. SMOCER. Our experience within the Financial Services Information Sharing and Analysis Center is that it does run the gamut from large to small. I would say the smaller organizations typically tend to be more consumers of the shared information. So in terms of protecting themselves, they tend to get the information that the larger institutions are witnessing in terms of attempted attacks, the nature of those attacks, consume that information, and then prepare to defend themselves better from that information.

I think one thing to recognize too is a lot of smaller institutions or organizations, be they in financial services or otherwise, are often supported by outside IT service providers. So I think one thing that is critical too in the information sharing debate is to make sure that those kind of service providers are engaged because they will help protect small institutions that they service.

Senator MORAN. That is a good point. The business that conducts business with a smaller business needs to be insistent upon the right framework in place for who they are contracting with.

Mr. SMOCER. And one of the advantages of the Framework for smaller businesses too is that in gauging the effectiveness of their service providers, they can use the Framework to ask the right questions of their service providers in a kind of lexicon that is common. We tend to think of the Framework as almost a Rosetta Stone in terms of taking a lot of disparate language around technology and cybersecurity and placing it in a common lexicon that service providers, customers, clients can understand.

Senator MORAN. And I would point out that while it may be an IT company that you are subcontracting or contracting with, a business contracts with lots of other businesses unrelated in a sense to IT, and there is an opportunity for the attack to occur there. And I do not know if this is demonstrated by facts yet today, but I assume that it may come to the point in which it is easier to attack the smaller business that contracts with a larger business and you arrive at the same point of very damaging occurrences. Does that make sense?

Mr. SMOCER. It does. And certainly in some of the examples that Senator Nelson was giving, in particular, one large retailer that was ostensibly attacked through a small HVAC provider.

Senator MORAN. Mr. England, just let me ask you why your company has the incentive to do what you are doing?

Mr. ENGLAND. It is a business imperative. You know, we talk about insurance as a protection against liability, but I like to think of the example of life insurance. It really does not benefit me if I am dead. And as a small business, I am dependent on the trust of my customers and being able to deliver them services in a secure environment. And as a small business, we could sustain probably just a small number of attacks before we would be—as a business entity, our going concern, would be in jeopardy. So there is a strong incentive to do that.

And I echo the comments that have been shared already that this is why we view it as a competitive advantage for us. We have had open conversations with larger companies that we are connecting to, and we have had open conversations with people who are providing services to us because it is a great risk.

Senator MORAN. Thank you very much.

Mr. Peters?

STATEMENT OF HON. GARY PETERS,
U.S. SENATOR FROM MICHIGAN

Senator PETERS. Thank you, Mr. Moran.

I really have enjoyed the testimony here and what is going to be an increasingly important discussion in the years ahead. And so I appreciate all of your involvement in this issue.

Mr. Lewis, if I can start with a question for you. In your testimony you, I think, very wisely said that the question is not how many folks are adopting the Framework. It is whether or not it is actually effective. And I think the jury is still out. It is still new. We are in the process of implementing it and companies are adopting it. So we will have more data points as we go forward. If you can kind of elaborate how we would assess that.

And in particular, you mentioned at the very end of your testimony too that you think this is a good start, but you also believe it is not enough. So where do you think we are going to be? We are going to have data points, obviously, to assess this. But where do we have to go that is even further than this Framework? What were you implying in your testimony?

Dr. LEWIS. Well, and thank you for the question.

The administration has chosen a voluntary approach, backed up by the implicit threat of regulatory action if companies do not do anything. And the jury is still out, as you said.

For me, the easiest way would be to just look at the number of incidents that we see, the losses that we see, and whether it is going up or down. And one of the ways I think about this is we have four or five primary opponents in cyberspace: the Russians who can pretty much do whatever they want, the Chinese who have a massive amount of resources, Iran and North Korea who have really improved in recent years, and the groups that Iran supports, some of the terrorist groups that Senator Nelson might be talking about. These are pros. Let us see how they react. Right? If their success rate goes down—and they have had an unbroken string of successes for more than a decade—then we can say we have done enough. But we do not have the data to say that.

If it is not enough, then we need to think where is it we want to take action to harden critical infrastructure and where is it we want to take action as a Government to work with these nation state opponents to get them to change their behavior.

So I think those are the two areas.

Watch the Framework. People have said they wanted to do voluntary stuff for a long time. Now is their chance. Prove that it works. If it does, great. But even if it works, there will still be a class of opponents who can only respond to Government action, and that is where we need to think.

Senator PETERS. Especially with the state actors is where we are going to need to do it.

Dr. LEWIS. Right.

Senator PETERS. Mr. Smocer, you mentioned in your testimony that you think that we could see a baseline of activity from companies based on insurance and insurance standards. And I also heard a number of folks comment that with regulation, you basically have a checklist process that you are going to go through.

How is it fundamentally different if it is an insurance company? Would an insurance company basically give you a checklist, say if you do these things, you will be insured? If you do not—what is the difference between those two approaches as you see it?

Mr. SMOCER. I would say that the way the Framework will be used is less about the checklist and more about underwriting the risk that the company faces. So I think as in any insurance, you need to have some level of standard underwriting and some lexicon that provides that to be able to get the actuary numbers to figure out the risk and figure out the premiums therefore that you are going to charge.

I think what the Framework does is it provides a really good risk framework that, as many of my colleagues have pointed out, is understandable from the board room down to the operations floor. And therefore, I think the insurance companies see this as an opportunity potentially to say this is the tool that we have been looking for to give us some standard underwriting guidance to be able to figure out our premiums and risk scenarios.

Senator PETERS. Thank you.

Mr. Romine, in your testimony you talked about your NICE initiative which deals with education because for us to effectively deal with this problem, we need folks who are highly skilled and trained in cybersecurity. Could you elaborate a little bit on what you talked about and how the initiative is progressing and what we need to do to make sure that we have the training programs in place to train folks who can deal with some of the threats from China and Russia and the others that are coming at us?

Dr. ROMINE. Certainly. Thank you, sir.

The NICE program that NIST is privileged to lead housing the national program office for NICE is actually a broad interagency activity. And it is focused on three things. One is cybersecurity awareness. One is fundamental education from K through post-graduate. And then related to that one is the development of a cybersecurity workforce, capable workforce.

And so the last one I think is the one that you are specifically interested in. And I would say a lot has been done in that space. There is a lot left to do. We have collaborated with the Department of Labor and the Office of Personnel Management, OPM, and others, the Department of Education, the National Science Foundation, and many of our other partners. And I think we are addressing some of the shortcomings associated with sort of understanding the needs, the requirements of that cybersecurity work force, the STEM education that is required to underpin a professional workforce in cybersecurity.

And so I think there is more to come. We still have a shortfall. This is, I think, well known. We need more capable cybersecurity actors. But we are making progress.

Senator MORAN. Mr. Schatz?

STATEMENT OF HON. BRIAN SCHATZ,
U.S. SENATOR FROM HAWAII

Senator SCHATZ. Thank you.

It seems all of the panelists emphasize—or at least most of the panelists emphasize that the voluntary nature of the Framework was key to its initial success. But I still believe there need to be quantifiable metrics to determine adoption among companies.

Can each of you briefly suggest more rigorous and precise ways to measure the adoption of the Framework beyond the October RFI?

Dr. ROMINE. I can start briefly and say that from NIST's perspective, it is the ongoing engagement with our industry partners. This is something that we did not deliver this to the President and walk away. We are actually continuing to engage. And what we are seeing is a shift in the conversation. The momentum is building.

Senator SCHATZ. But you are a data person. So what are going to be the metrics? I mean, that sounds like me talking. Let us talk about what are the metrics for success for those programs.

Dr. ROMINE. I represent a measurement institute, and so this is something that we take very, very seriously. Of course, one of the problems that you have to worry about is you can sometimes get what you measure if you are not careful about designing the measurements.

We are still trying to figure out exactly the appropriate approach for measuring the rate or the level of use of the Framework. But I think——

Senator SCHATZ. So we do not have metrics yet.

Dr. ROMINE. We do not yet. The Framework is still—as we have pointed out, it is kind of in its infancy. It is less than a year old, and I think the amount of momentum is pretty striking given that fact of its youth. But we are working on ways that we can try to assess this.

Senator SCHATZ. What is your time-frame for developing metrics and reporting back to the Congress on progress?

Dr. ROMINE. I would be reluctant to give you a very specific time, but I can tell you we are diligently working on trying to determine the best approach for measuring that.

Senator SCHATZ. Ms. Beauchesne?

Ms. BEAUCHESNE. Well, I am not from a metrics institute. But I will tell you I would think about it this way. Everyone wears seatbelts now. People do not smoke now. I think we need a campaign like that. And when we start to see people around the country understanding we are talking about the cyber Framework, that it is not just a big news story when they hit a Federal department or one of our big retailers, everyone understands what it means to protect your networks and what good cyber hygiene means, then that will be success.

Mr. SMOCER. And I approach it from a slightly different perspective coming from an industry that already has a fair amount of cybersecurity regulation associated with it. I mean, our concern is primarily around assuring that our members are aware of it. And part of the way we are doing that, by the way, is through some survey information that we are doing. So through the FSISAC, the Information Sharing and Analysis Center, through the sector coordinating council that we have, we have done an awareness survey, and we know that the institutions are very aware of it. We are then probably going to move on to kind of what the usage is.

Our big concern, though, is reconciling the Framework with the existing regulatory structure that we have.

Mr. ENGLAND. I do not have the same kind of national reach that my colleagues do here to get that kind of visibility. But I can just share with you my own personal experience.

This year, we have, independent from all this, gone through a review of our whole vendor management process. And as we have gone through that, we realized that this would perhaps be an ideal opportunity to ask some critical questions about cybersecurity. And in particular, we have included a question as to whether or not our vendors and suppliers, those we partner with, are using the NIST Cybersecurity Framework.

I think, as Ms. Beauchesne pointed out, the more conversations that we are having about this, the more dialogues that we are having with those that we interface with on our systems—and we are seeing more interest growing in it and more conversations surrounding it as a result. And so I think it is an organic growth.

Senator SCHATZ. Dr. Lewis?

Dr. LEWIS. Thank you.

I would call everyone's attention to section 10 of the Executive Order which says that if the voluntary measures do not work, the White House reserves the right to do more in a regulatory fashion. They did an assessment of the effectiveness of the Framework a few months after it came out. Amazingly enough, they found that it was succeeding. I do not know how they figured that out.

We have multiple data sources and we need to use them all. The sector-specific agencies that oversee critical infrastructure sectors need to collect data on the status of these companies and how many times they have been hacked.

Senator SCHATZ. And is it NIST's job to aggregate all of those data, or is there a lead Government agency? You mentioned the FBI going to a company. But is there a point agency on aggregating all of these data?

Dr. LEWIS. There is not, and that might be a useful thing. I think NIST is not really the aggregator here. NIST could come up with standards for aggregation. FBI statistics are useful. Just the number of times they have sent people out to notify companies, which was in the thousands in the last 2 years.

Senator SCHATZ. But right now there is no lead Federal Government agency in terms of getting our arms around the problem.

Dr. LEWIS. No. DHS does not have the authority nor do they have the sources. The intelligence community collects data on foreign success rates. That data is classified, but I would suggest that we are not doing so well. DOD collects information on the defense industrial base. And finally, Commerce has some authorities they have not taken advantage of.

Senator SCHATZ. OK. Thank you. My time is up.

The CHAIRMAN [presiding]. Senator Daines?

STATEMENT OF HON. STEVE DAINES,
U.S. SENATOR FROM MONTANA

Senator DAINES. Thank you, Mr. Chairman.

Prior to coming up here and starting this new day job, I spent 28 years in the private sector. So I am always one that hopes to see more private sector-led solutions here. In fact, I was 12 years as exec in a cloud computing company, and it was always in our best interest to make sure we had our networks hardened and always had the best practices on cybersecurity because if we failed to do so, we did not have a business any longer.

Mr. Romine, a question for you. This Framework was released about a year ago, February 12, 2014, version 1.0. How long did it take from kind of the beginnings of the process to put together V1.0 here before it released?

Dr. ROMINE. It took the full year. We were given a year by the executive order. The first request for information that we asked the private sector to react was immediately after the release of the executive order. We subsequently needed to engage all of the stakeholders, private sector, Government regulators, industry associations, and international community over the course of the next year in five separate workshops that were held geographically distributed around the country. On the basis of that feedback, after an initial release of a draft, we subsequently amended the draft, and the version that you see that was given to the President on schedule, I am proud to say, was the culmination of that year's effort.

Senator DAINES. So round numbers, it is about 2 years old I guess as we sit here today, from the beginning of the process to where we are at today.

Dr. ROMINE. That is correct.

Senator DAINES. You probably had your beta release, and then you have got your version 1.0 here.

Dr. ROMINE. Yes, sir.

Senator DAINES. I know as we were building our company—one of our strategic advantages—we could run faster than anybody else. That is how we won in the technology space. And we grew a large company. We capitalized nearly $2 billion from virtually starting up from nowhere. I mean, I have lived in the world here of data and cloud computing.

But I am just wondering how current now, given the speed at which the bad guys are moving, given the start about 2 years ago— you know, when is version 2.0 to come out, and how often do you see updating the standard?

Dr. ROMINE. Thank you, sir.

I think it is important to note that the Framework is not technology-specific. That is, we are not trying to institute specific technologies that are going to be out of date almost as soon as a document appears. Instead, it describes a process, a framework that you can use to communicate your cybersecurity needs both internally, as well as with external stakeholders. And so I do not think that is something that will—even though this is a fast-moving area, I—

——

Senator DAINES. I see that. It is clearly a framework and a process that is laid out here in terms of assessing risk and so forth.

Dr. ROMINE. That is right.

Senator DAINES. One thing I also notice about D.C.—this is a town that seems to reward activity and not results. How do you help companies try to quantify this process in terms of eventually the outcome? We have moved this process here, but they have got to put, I think, some kind of quantitative assessment whether it is a 0 to 100 scale, whether it is a letter scale to say—and I have a question for Mr. England too. If you say are they complying with NIST, what does that mean?

Dr. ROMINE. I can just start by saying as part of the Framework, in fact, there is an evaluation of the level of assurance that an organization has that they are responding to the various functions that are listed in the Framework, the so-called tiers that we have developed. And so there is an internal assessment capability already.

With regard to helping businesses, particularly small and medium businesses, we have active engagement. We have outreach that predates the development of the Framework, and we are now using those outreach mechanisms with trade associations, with small businesses throughout the country to socialize the Framework, to increase awareness.

Senator DAINES. One thing I think is helpful, I guess, is, is there a way to try to grade, assess, quantify what it means to have adopted this Framework, I think moving in that direction, so there is a way to have a comparative analysis between company A or company B?

Dr. ROMINE. I think it depends. It is a little bit dangerous to go that route principally because the companies face different contexts of use, and so comparing across is going to be very challenging. I think the internal assessment of how effective your cybersecurity enterprise or your risk management approach is——

Senator DAINES. That is probably the better question in terms of looking—it is a continuum here in a rapidly very dynamic—you know, rapidly changing environment. If we start here, we do this assessment, 6 months later or a year later, we can see if we are making progress or not. I think it probably is some value add.

And last, what I see too—I will know when these are being used when something like this has got its—you can tell it is not just sitting on the shelf and gathering dust. I am just always a little skeptical of this town where they just want to create some activity. We got a standard and here it is. And the real question will be adoption and focusing whether we want more of this. It is like bread. If it is fresh, they are going to want it. If it gets stale, it will just be another binder on the bookshelf.

Dr. ROMINE. I could not agree more. We heard universally from all of our stakeholders that more shelf-ware was not what was needed, and I think we took that into account in engaging broadly across the stakeholder interests and listening to their concerns and developing, in conjunction with the stakeholders, a document that is actually usable.

Senator DAINES. All right. Thank you. I am out of time.

The CHAIRMAN. Thank you, Senator Daines.

Senator Klobuchar?

STATEMENT OF HON. AMY KLOBUCHAR,
U.S. SENATOR FROM MINNESOTA

Senator KLOBUCHAR. Thank you very much, Mr. Chairman.

Thank you everyone. Mr. Smocer, please say hello to Governor Pawlenty, my friend, who I know is, I guess, your boss.

Mr. SMOCER. He is in fact my boss.

Senator KLOBUCHAR. Is he doing OK?

Mr. SMOCER. Yes.

[Laughter.]

Mr. SMOCER. No. He is doing very well.

Senator KLOBUCHAR. All right. Very good.

And then also I think you mentioned the major retailer who was attacked, and of course, I think everyone knows that was Target out of Minnesota. So we have seen firsthand the devastating effect this can have even though there was not a lot of actual damage to consumers, but what happened to Target because of that, even though they were in fact victims of theft. And we are proud that they have come back from that.

But I think we all know the effect that this has on companies and on consumers. And I just think there is a moment here, maybe because of what happened with Sony and other things, where there might be a space to actually move forward on some legislation which, as we all know, crosses many committees. And I happen to be on two of them, Commerce as well as Judiciary, where I think we can move forward.

I was going to ask you, Mr. Romine, just if you could answer briefly, if there are any industries you think are ahead of this that are doing better jobs than others in terms of taking this on.

Dr. ROMINE. We have certainly had active engagement from a number of sectors. The ones who are the most, I think, critically dependent upon information technology have had kind of a head start on cybersecurity issues, and so the financial services sector certainly is a leading sector in that area. I think the energy sector—some of the regulated industries, industries that have had to cope with regulation overall, I think have also kind of had a little bit of a head start.

Senator KLOBUCHAR. And could you explain how the Framework is going to be technology-neutral? I know there have been some concerns raised about overly complex regulations.

Dr. ROMINE. That is right.

Senator KLOBUCHAR. Can you explain in a not complex way?

Dr. ROMINE. I will do my best.

The Framework itself is completely technology agnostic. It does not specify any particular technologies. It just talks about standards and best practices. And I should point out that the Framework is actually predicated on use of existing bodies of standards, many of them international. And I think it is an important thing to note that that gives greater opportunity to harmonize things, particularly for multinational corporations who have a difficult time responding to different regulatory environments in different parts of the globe.

Senator KLOBUCHAR. Ms. Beauchesne, I know the Chamber has been working with law enforcement, you know, FBI, Secret Service, cops on the beat. I used to be a prosecutor for 8 years, and at the beginnings of this, I cannot tell you what this was like. We had line officers that would show up at a house that had some cyber problem and turn on the computer and all the evidence would vanish because someone had set it up that way. And I know there has been more training in law enforcement, and certainly as you get to the upper levels, there is more training.

Is the working relationship good? How do you think this can move forward in terms of making sure we are doing a better job in being as sophisticated as the crooks that are taking our private data?

Ms. BEAUCHESNE. That is a very good question. Thank you.

I think that, again, keeping this Framework flexible, keeping it non-regulatory so that we can move at the speed of the bad guys is essential.

As far as law enforcement, I think the relationship is very good. When we have gone around the country doing the Chamber's Cyber Campaign, we have included the local FBI and the local Secret Service person so that our members in Austin, Texas, for instance, get to meet them, get to have face time with them so that when something does happen, they know where to go.

And I would also say at the Bureau, we now have a private sector office, a private sector lead there. So our members have one-stop shopping and know where to go. So I think it is a good relationship.

Senator KLOBUCHAR. Very good.

My last question is actually for anyone that wants to chime in. Senator Blunt and I successfully included an amendment to make sure that NIST was accountable in the process in terms of getting us information on what is happening.

But my question is the President talked about information sharing and liability protection legislation as an important incentive to encourage further participation in both the NIST Framework and other cybersecurity efforts. I guess I would ask the panel, especially from the private sector side, how important is this for moving forward.

Mr. SMOCER. Sure. I think we were certainly very encouraged by the comments because I think the liability protection is a key component that we have been looking for. I think we would love to see that extended. In the Framework, the recommendation—it was mainly private-to-government that would be covered by the liability protection. We think that needs to extend a bit to the private-to-private sharing models as well. You know, a lot of times——

Senator KLOBUCHAR. Are there like antitrust concerns? You know, if you start giving data to your competitors saying something is happening in terms of the liability issues you are worried about.

Mr. SMOCER. Well, I think if I were a GC, that might be one of the reasons I would discourage information sharing. But I think in reality the recognition is this—when it comes to cybersecurity, this largely has to be a noncompetitive issue because the reality is that any institution that gets attacked is probably witnessing the next victim's circumstance. So if we can share that information more freely with the right protections in place, I think that is very important.

Senator KLOBUCHAR. Anyone else?

Ms. BEAUCHESNE. If I could just add on the information sharing piece. Absolutely, the liability protections are absolutely essential for the private sector. Whether it is FOIA, whether it is regulatory, the antitrust, businesses need those safeguards in order to share that information. We do not want to be blaming the victim. We want the companies to be able to share that information with impunity.

Senator KLOBUCHAR. All right. Thank you very much.

The CHAIRMAN. Thank you, Senator Klobuchar.

Senator Manchin has returned.

STATEMENT OF HON. JOE MANCHIN,
U.S. SENATOR FROM WEST VIRGINIA

Senator MANCHIN. Thank you so much, Mr. Chairman. I am so sorry because we've got two or three meetings going on. I would hate to look like it is being rude, but we are not. We are just trying to make all of our meetings.

Let me just say this to all of you. I want to thank you all for your service and also being here and helping us through these most difficult situations.

To Mr. Romine, you first, sir. The West Virginia National Guard is partnering with the University of Charleston and the Blue Ridge Technical College on a cyber training program that will help address the workforce shortage issues that are highlighted in the roadmap for improving critical infrastructure cybersecurity. The West Virginia National Guard and the University of Charleston have also developed undergraduate and graduate-level cybersecurity certificate programs based on the national training standards.

How is your office and the National Initiative for Cybersecurity Education coordinating with the West Virginia National Guard on this program and what can we do, all of us and yourself, better to support innovative partnerships like this?

Dr. ROMINE. Thank you, Senator. We are certainly always pleased when there are organizations that are taking this very seriously and developing curricula and contributing to solving the workforce issue. I do not have any specifics about that particular case except that I would say we would be delighted to engage and have discussion.

Senator MANCHIN. Do you all have the ability to partner up with them to help them take these programs to higher levels, or how does that work?

Dr. ROMINE. We certainly have the ability to contribute and share ideas under our program.

Senator MANCHIN. So I can get them in contact with you to make sure we can hook up?

Dr. ROMINE. I would welcome that.

Senator MANCHIN. Ms. Beauchesne, banks and other financial institutions are already responsible for following a variety of regulations related to cybersecurity. They have requirements to protect against breaches, as well as requirements about how to respond in the event of a breach. They could be responsible for cyber theft that occurs through a third party even if the threat was not the fault of the bank.

If financial institutions continue to bear the financial liability for cyber attacks, what incentive will other industries, such as retail, have to invest in voluntary cybersecurity protections?

And they are starting to move a piece of legislation saying, listen, somebody else has to have skin in the game. If it is not my fault and you will not invest, whether it be—I am using Target, and maybe they have done everything possible. But it was a tremendous breach. But basically it fell on the responsibility of the banks.

I have been called personally. They said your credit card has been jeopardized, and we want you to cut it up. We will send you a new one. I have had that done twice now.

So with all that being done, the banks are saying we would not have to have this if they are doing everything possible.

So two things. What can they do, and do you think that it should be a dual responsibility? Whoever is at fault may have not done what technology would allow them to do. Should the institution, whether it be commercial or retail, bear the brunt?

Ms. BEAUCHESNE. Yes. I think that the brunt should be shared by all involved.

Senator MANCHIN. Do you think legislation would be needed to share that rather than the financial sector taking the full brunt?

Ms. BEAUCHESNE. I am not completely familiar with the legislation, so I will not commit to that.

But what I would say is we are——

Senator MANCHIN. It is pretty simple. Who pays? Who did wrong and who pays?

Ms. BEAUCHESNE. I think we are going to see a sharing of who pays. I think that you are seeing companies step up, and here is why because it is not just about who pays. They want to protect their customers. They want to protect their brand, and it is in their interest to do so.

Senator MANCHIN. I know they want to, but when they know that it is not going to cost them anything when it is breached and they have not stepped up and bought the latest and greatest technology to try to develop it and work, what is their incentive to do so? And you are going to have to convince all of us that we need to step in there and say, OK, you are at fault, you pay.

Anybody else want to comment on this? I see Mr. Lewis down there shaking his head.

Dr. LEWIS. So I talked to the head of a major credit card company, and what he said to me is, you know, it is a problem for us, but if I put a nickel on your credit card bill, are you going to notice. And that will cover the expenses. So everyone in the room who has a credit card, you are paying 5 or 10 cents a year, and that covers fraud.

The debate is over two things. First, the cost is going up, and you may start to notice when you are paying more, and that is where you are getting companies saying, hey, wait a minute. Why am I holding responsibility for this?

Senator MANCHIN. You are talking about the financial companies, financial institutions.

Dr. LEWIS. Yes, because currently they bear the liability, and they would like not to.

Senator MANCHIN. I am just saying the innovative and creative ideas will come if you make me responsibility and hold me liable. I will push the demographics, if you will, if I know that it could fall back on me. If not, I might be a little complacent, saying you know what, Mr. Eamon here is going to have to pay it, so I am not worried. I have done all I can. I do not need to do anymore. I am not going to incur that much more expense.

Dr. LEWIS. We did a study of major breaches and what we found is the first phase is the bad guys get in. The second phase is they are discovered, and the third phase is everyone points at everyone else and says they are responsible. So some allocation of responsibility would be good.

Senator MANCHIN. Thank you, Mr. Chairman. I am sorry.

The CHAIRMAN. Thank you, Senator Manchin.

Next up as we move west, Senator Udall.

STATEMENT OF HON. TOM UDALL, U.S. SENATOR FROM NEW MEXICO

Senator UDALL. Thank you very much, Chairman Thune, and great to be back with you on the Commerce Committee. And I am going to talk a little bit about a couple of things we have worked on in the past.

Today American citizens, businesses, and government agencies face what I think are very serious cyber threats, and so I really appreciate this hearing. Everything from personal data, to trade secrets, to national security are at risk from intrusion by independent hackers and foreign governments. They even tell me our own Senate offices are frequently the subject of those kinds of attacks from foreign governments. Cyber threats are real and can cripple our water systems, our oil pipelines, and hospitals, and I think we need to take these threats very seriously.

I have supported cybersecurity legislation in the Senate, including the Rockefeller and Thune Cybersecurity Enhancement Act that became law, I believe in the last Congress. I support measures to improve our cybersecurity defense, including important work at two national laboratories in my home state of New Mexico. Los Alamos National Laboratory is a leader in quantum cryptography, and Sandia National Laboratory is engaged in efforts to secure the national electrical grid from cyber attack. Sandia has partnerships with universities and the private sector. They are helping computer science students become cyber professionals.

And when I look at this field, like many Americans, I also have a lot of concerns about what our own Government is doing in terms of domestic surveillance. And I think it is absolutely clear we need to strike the right balance between security and our civil liberties. But I know that is not the main focus here.

So, Dr. Romine, I would like to ask you about the subject of cloud computing. Your testimony briefly notes that NIST plays a role for advancing standards for cloud computing. Senator Moran and I worked on a piece of legislation, which was signed into law last year, called the Federal IT Acquisition Reform Act. And we know from the GAO that smarter Federal IT policies could lead to billions of dollars in taxpayer savings. This includes greater use of cloud computing across the Federal Government.

So I would like to ask what is NIST's vision with respect to cloud computing. What does NIST see as the primary challenges for cybersecurity when it comes to cloud computing, and how is NIST working with other Federal agencies to support their transition to the cloud?

Dr. ROMINE. Thank you, Senator.

NIST has been involved in cloud computing. We have an ongoing cloud computing research program and standards program today in my laboratory, the Information Technology Laboratory. We engaged with other Federal stakeholders during the development of the FedRAMP process which is based on standards that we developed in consultation with the private sector again. Our standard MO is to work with the private sector on these issues. We establish the basic definitions for cloud computing.

With regard to cybersecurity, one of the challenges, of course—cloud computing has sort of a multi-tendency component to it, meaning that multiple people are on the same hardware at the same time, and there is the potential for sort of bleeding over. So we have to be careful about that.

But another issue and one that we have just issued guidance about has to do with cloud forensics. That is, given that you are no longer necessarily just local in your IT space but rather using a cloud provider, how do you after the fact figure out what happened using forensics techniques. And so we have got some recent guidance that we have issued on that.

Senator UDALL. I do not know if any of the other panelists have any comment on what he was talking about. You all are good on that?

You noticed and you talked about working with the private sector. Is NIST getting the level of cooperation it needs from industry stakeholders?

Dr. ROMINE. I think the level of engagement has been astonishing. We have been very pleased at the number of people who have engaged with us both in terms of responding to requests for information in the early processes of Framework development, for example, as well as 6 months after or 8 months after the Framework was released, information about how it is being used and the lessons that we can learn. That response has been tremendous. The workshop engagement has been fantastic. So we are very excited.

Senator UDALL. Thank you very much.

And thank you, Chairman Thune.

The CHAIRMAN. Thank you, Senator Udall.

Senator Gardner is up next.

STATEMENT OF HON. CORY GARDNER, U.S. SENATOR FROM COLORADO

Senator GARDNER. Thank you, Mr. Chairman. Thanks for holding this hearing as well, and thank you to the witnesses for being here today and your testimony.

I had an opportunity about 6 months ago to visit one of the largest tech employers in Colorado, manufacturing. They focus a lot on security issues, focus a lot on issues dealing with servers around the country, around the world really looking for, I guess, attacks, aberrations in terms of what is happening to their systems. And it was an interesting point that they made. They had said something to me to the effect of we no longer are just assuming that we will be able to prevent and keep out these attacks, but we have to assume that the attacks have been made, that somebody has made it inside. And now we are just trying to figure out how to keep them out of everything else and I guess cordon them off, so to speak, into an area where it does no harm.

Do you think that is an accurate way to look at the world of technology today, Dr. Romine?

Dr. ROMINE. I think in most conversations with cybersecurity professionals, you will find that there is no discussion that we will be 100 percent successful at keeping people out of our systems. And so what I think has to happen is an understanding of sort of where the crown jewels are regardless of, whether you are the Federal Government or whether private sector, what sector that you are in, and then seek additional steps to ensure that the very serious— whether it is proprietary information, whether it is personally identifiable information, those kinds of assets have to have special protection.

Senator GARDNER. And obviously, you do a lot of work at the NIST lab, whether it is NTIA work, telecommunications work, the atomic clock, things like GPS, and other issues. And this Framework which you believe is and will always be voluntary—is that correct?

Dr. ROMINE. Yes, sir.

Senator GARDNER. The other question I have is if you have this Framework, you have set this Framework up, you have agreement, how do you define success. What is success 5 years out from now with the Framework in place?

Dr. ROMINE. I think one of the perhaps useful analogies here is if you take a look at the evolution of safety programs in the private sector, for example, they initiated with let us do the following things. This is a checklist of things in order to ensure that we are trying to have a safe environment. And that was sort of all you did.

Over the course of decades I think, there has been a move from that to baking safety into everything that you do operationally, and I think the same thing is going to happen here. The culture is going to change. One year into the Framework, we are not expecting a complete culture shift, but we are seeing signs that the conversations that need to take place between suppliers and between components of an organization and the executives—those conversations are taking place or beginning to take place. So I think the more pervasive that becomes, I think the more we have confidence that people are taking seriously the need to secure their networks and their systems and information.

Senator GARDNER. Ms. Beauchesne and perhaps Mr. England might be able to address the next question. Ms. Beauchesne, in your testimony you talked about making incentives work. You talked about liability issues. You talked about leveraging Federal procurements, making research and development tax credit permanent, those kinds of things. Are there currently private sector incentives to achieve these cybersecurity needs and making sure that we are bolstering and doing everything we can to prevent attacks or vulnerabilities?

And I guess what I mean by that is this. Is simply the cost of an attack so great that that provides the incentive? Are banks that are looking to make loans to companies looking at cybersecurity and saying we believe that you present too much of a risk for us to make a loan and therefore the interest rate is going to be higher or lower because you have done such a good job. Are there ISO ratings that you could look at and say this is a NIST standard of security that we believe is necessary in order to people to carry out their function without risk?

Ms. BEAUCHESNE. I think what you said is right. They want to do the right thing—right—because the risks are so high, the costs of doing business. They have to do the right thing.

But the other piece of that I think is we need to look at especially the small and medium-sized companies that are being attacked by nation states. I mean, that is costly to protect against. The Framework is not going to do that. If we had every company in the country adopt the Framework, that still would not prevent the Chinese or the Russians or whomever from attacking our companies. So I do think incentives are out there.

That is not our biggest push, if you will. I mean, we want the information sharing legislation. Incentives exist. We are looking at the Safety Act. We are looking at insurance. But the bottom line is we want the Framework to remain flexible, non-regulatory, and let us get that information sharing piece done.

Senator GARDNER. And are you satisfied, Dr. Romine—in my question and answer that it will remain voluntary. Are you satisfied with that?

Ms. BEAUCHESNE. From everything I hear, yes.

Senator GARDNER. Mr. England?

Mr. ENGLAND. I mean, in terms of incentives, we do not really look into the equation in terms of what the cost of a breach might be because with the size of our business as a small business, our costs are far greater. If we have breaches that displace the trust of our customers and the people that we connect to, our ability to continue as a going concern for a business is what our risk is. So the incentives are there because there is an inherent business imperative to do it.

And it is one of the reasons why I have been a big proponent of the Framework and the voluntary nature of it because when you start throwing into it some of these regulated pieces—as Ms. Beauchesne mentioned, the threat is ever-evolving, and so we have to have a tool and a mechanism that is ever-evolving as well and allow for adaptation as we go because the problem with the regulation side of it—and, of course, it depends on how it is written, but it is not a I go through this, I determine that I have met some minimum standard or minimum requirement, and I am done because you will never be done.

And so for us, our incentive actually is to be here today and to petition against the regulation because, to be quite honest with you, anything that would be regulated as minimum standard requirements is not going to be enough. And so we are going to have to do our own activities above and beyond that anyway in order to maintain our systems the way that we want. And so what is going to happen is it is actually going to be more costly for us to implement cybersecurity activities in our organization because we are following a dual track, what the regulating body wants and what the market demands.

Senator GARDNER. Thank you.

Thank you, Mr. Chairman.

The CHAIRMAN. Thank you, Senator Gardner.

Senator Blumenthal?

STATEMENT OF HON. RICHARD BLUMENTHAL, U.S. SENATOR FROM CONNECTICUT

Senator BLUMENTHAL. Thank you, Mr. Chairman, and thank you for holding this hearing and making it a priority because, as we know on both sides of the aisle and as one of our military leaders has said, and I am sure it has been repeated here, that the next Pearl Harbor may well be a cyber attack. Sony was certainly a sign that we ignore, at our grave peril, that a cyberattack may be the method of choice for aggressors who mean to do harm to our country.

And my view is that we are patently vulnerable at the moment, and I think the testimony this morning has reinforced my view that this Nation must do better. We are susceptible now by choice. It is not an accident. It is not something that we cannot anticipate. It is by choice that we are, in effect, failing to address this peril before it hits us. And I believe there needs to be greater Government direction and legislative involvement.

For the moment the best and most immediate response is for the private sector to do more with the encouragement and incentives that Government can provide. And as you know, as directed by the Government's Executive Order on Cybersecurity, the Secretaries of Homeland Security, Commerce, and Treasury were required to provide a report to the White House on how the Government can best provide those kinds of incentives to participate in the Framework, especially for smaller businesses.

And I am very concerned about the impact on smaller businesses because the effect on a Sony eventually becomes an effect on smaller businesses; just as the effect on a defense contractor becomes an effect on the suppliers and components makers and so forth that we see in manufacturing submarines or the Joint Strike Fighter or helicopters, which we make in Connecticut. So I am interested in what progress has been made in developing better incentives.

Dr. Lewis, as you alluded to in your testimony, it appears there may have been a lack of incentives on the part of many companies to make the right decisions about cybersecurity. So let me ask you. What were your thoughts on the recommended incentives that agencies made to the President following the executive order? Did any of these ideas particularly impress you as being effective?

Dr. LEWIS. Thank you for the question.

I would note in general that I think this program will remain voluntary until there are too many incidents to ignore. And we are approaching that. We have got a lot of people who do not like us out there in the world, and they are very active in cyberspace because it is so easy.

The problem with the incentives is really it has to be legislation. It has to be the Congress that creates incentives because incentives are either regulatory relief, tax relief, or some kind of money. And if you do not have those three things, it really is not that much of an incentive. It is not enough.

Senator BLUMENTHAL. So, in effect, what I hear you saying is that the President's executive order will be a nullity unless the Congress acts.

Dr. LEWIS. I think that legislation of some kind is necessary. I think the White House decided in 2012 to move ahead because of the problems then with legislation, but I know that they would probably welcome adequate legislation that would strengthen authorities and create incentives such as liability protection.

Senator BLUMENTHAL. So at a time when, rightly or wrongly, there has been criticism of the President for, in effect, usurping authority through executive order, here is an area where clearly legislation is necessary to accomplish the goals that we all believe are absolutely requisite at this point in our history.

Dr. LEWIS. Having followed the development of the executive order pretty closely, I think that everyone would agree that this is an area where Congress has to take the lead. Congress has to legislate.

Senator BLUMENTHAL. Dr. Romine, let me ask you in the time I have remaining. One idea that has been discussed is that Federal agencies develop a "certificate of compliance" or some other sort of identifier much like the Energy Star system, which is in a way a seal of approval to recognize the companies that are proven to be observing guidelines laid out in the NIST Framework.

How could NIST be helpful in a process like that one? Do you think there is anything that would prevent NIST from working with Federal agencies to provide some certificate of compliance, which would be a strong incentive or encouragement for companies, in effect, to protect themselves more adequately?

Dr. ROMINE. Thank you, Senator.

I am not sure that having NIST play both the role of participating in partnership with the private sector and then coming behind and doing some sort of an audit would preserve our ability to work collaboratively with those folks.

The other thing I will say with regard to incentives, although some of the discussion has surrounded incentives where there are market failures, I think we also have to recognize the inherent market incentives that are being made evident. One is, of course, managing the overall risk, in particular your reputational risk, and there have been companies that have been singled out here as victims of hacking, and that is problematic for them. When you become known in that way, it is a serious reputational risk, and I think there are some incentives to avoid that.

The other incentives involve the burgeoning development of the insurance industry, cybersecurity insurance that is beginning to be underpinned by some of the work that went into the Framework.

Senator BLUMENTHAL. Well, I would just say in closing—and my time has expired—they paid a price, a reputational price, as well as enormous costs to their business, whether it is Target or Sony, and some of the individuals have paid a personal price, individuals in command of the companies. But that price all too often is one that is shared among innocent parties, companies that are linked to that one, consumers who pay a higher price whether it is through insurance or the charges that are passed on. So eventually failure to protect themselves has a cost that is societal and economic spread broadly throughout the Nation and that is why we are here today.

Thank you, Mr. Chairman.

The CHAIRMAN. Thank you, Senator Blumenthal.

I am going to ask a couple of quick questions here. I think everybody else—unless we check with my colleagues here if they want to have a second round.

Dr. Romine, NIST also plays a role in certain technical aspects of information sharing under its existing FISMA statutory authority. The NIST draft guide to cyber threat information sharing released recently provides guidance for an organization's coordinated computer security incident handling.

So question number one is, what feedback has NIST received from stakeholders regarding the guide and how will the final version recognize the different approaches for cyber threat information sharing being used in the public and private sectors?

Dr. ROMINE. Thank you, Mr. Chairman.

The release of Special Publication 800–150, which you refer to, has gotten a lot of feedback. The feedback has been robust. The time for feedback I think closed just this past November, and we are dispositioning those comments now.

I think it is important to note that again the guidance that we have provided is technology agnostic. We talk about various different approaches. Our role, as you correctly pointed out, is the sort of standards for the kind of information exchange that is envisioned, this information sharing.

And it is important to point out we want to ensure that that information sharing is done in a way that is standard and interoperable principally because we want to have computers be able to ingest that information and act on it in sort of network speed instead of just sharing information. I think sometimes people talk about information sharing currently as being phone calls from network operators that happen to know each other, and I think we want to get well beyond that into a much more integrated approach.

The CHAIRMAN. Do you believe NIST ought to have a role in providing additional guidance on cyber threat information sharing by non-Federal entities?

Dr. ROMINE. I think we are very comfortable with the role that we have today, the standards and guidelines and best practices for information sharing, as well as the work that we have done to underpin security automation, which is what I alluded to just now.

With regard to the private sector, I think that is much more of a policy issue and something I do not think would be necessarily appropriate for us to engage in.

The CHAIRMAN. You mentioned in your testimony that tech companies have been developing products and services aligned with the Framework. Are there any examples of those types of products and services you can share with us?

Dr. ROMINE. I could do that. I am not prepared to do it today, but I am happy to provide the Committee with some of these products and services that are beginning to be developed.

The CHAIRMAN. Senator Gardner, anything else? All right.

Well, we have got a few things. We will keep the hearing record open for a couple weeks for members to submit any additional questions for the record, and I will probably have a few of those myself.

But I appreciate very much the great job of our panel today. Thank you not only for your remarks but also for your responses to our questions. It is an issue of great importance on so many levels to our country, and it is important that we get it right. Your expertise and counsel will be very important in helping shape the decisions that we make here. So thank you for that.

And with that, this hearing is adjourned.

[Whereupon, at 11:46 a.m., the hearing was adjourned.]

APPENDIX

PREPARED STATEMENT OF JOSHUA J. PAULI, PH.D., ASSOCIATE PROFESSOR OF CYBER SECURITY, DAKOTA STATE UNIVERSITY

ON IMPLEMENTATION OF S. 1353: CYBERSECURITY ENHANCEMENT ACT OF 2014

It is with great honor that I submit this testimony in support of the Cybersecurity Enhancement Act of 2014 and to share my professional opinion on how to best implement specific portions of the Act. As one of the lead cybersecurity faculty members at Dakota State University (DSU) in Madison, SD, I am deeply interested and invested in any legislation that affects the future of cybersecurity education. Dakota State University (DSU) is one of the leading institutions of higher education in the Nation in the area of cybersecurity, where we are designated as one of only 13 institutions in the Nation as a National Security Agency (NSA) Center of Academic Excellence (CAE) in Cyber Operations. The NSA and Department of Homeland Security (DHS) have also designate DSU as a CAE in Information Assurance Education and a CAE in Information Assurance Research. We currently have over 500 students studying cyber security at the bachelors, masters, and doctorate level.

Assisting Senator Thune's office during the last 18 months on this piece of legislation has given me an opportunity to see the detailed goals, proposed implementation, and intended outcomes of this Act come into focus. Now that the Act has been signed into law, it is critical that we identify the most appropriate ways to ensure the success of the legislation. The most applicable way to ensure the level of success that we all hope for is to leverage existing mechanisms and models that have a proven track record of success as much as we can. This will ensure we don't "reinvent the wheel", and instead provide funding and support to programs that we already trust and are currently reaping the benefits from.

One example of this in this Act is the inclusion, by name, of the National Science Foundation's Scholarship for Service (NSF–SFS) CyberCorps program in Section 302. The positive outcomes from this NSF program cannot be argued and there is certainly universal support for the continued and expanded support of it. As the Primary Investigator for DSU's NSF–SFS CyberCorps program, I can provide firsthand evidence of the success of the program as many of my colleagues around the Nation at other NSF–SFS CyberCorps institutions would as well. It is one of the driving forces in making DSU a cybersecurity leader in higher education. I applaud you for its inclusion in the Act and encourage you to continue to increase its funding level in future years, as it's truly a "best bang for buck".

Along these lines, I would like call your attention to TITLE III—EDUCATION AND WORKFORCE DEVELOPMENT and specifically SEC. 301. CYBERSECURITY COMPETITIONS AND CHALLENGES. Creating and holding cybersecurity competitions and challenges that help identify the next wave of cyber professionals are activities that have long been conducted by colleges and universities in partnership with NSF, DHS, NSA, and others. One current Federal program that fits perfectly with this goal of the Act is NSA's Center of Academic Excellence in Cyber Operations that started in 2012. This designation program aims to partner with institutions of higher education around the Nation that have academic degree programs that match, almost verbatim, to the *(d) Areas of Skill* included in the Act:

(1) ethical hacking;

(2) penetration testing;

(3) vulnerability assessment;

(4) continuity of system operations;

(5) security in design;

(6) cyber forensics;

(7) offensive and defensive cyber operations;

The NSA's CAE in Cyber Operations program can help implement curriculum, competitions, workshops, and related assistance in these exact seven areas. Without a doubt, any educational efforts dedicated to these areas should not only include this NSA program, but I strongly encourage you to have the NSA lead any efforts related to these specific areas of skill. By doing so, you're not only directly leveraging the NSA's knowledge and expertise, but more importantly, you would then have a direct pathway to the designated institutions across the Nation that are already working in this exact domain. The NSA and these 13 institutions already have a working structure and model to take on these type of projects and deliver them back out to the greater community in a timely and cost-effective manner.

Section 301 also includes *(b) Participation* that includes *(1) students enrolled in grades 9 through 12.* This is another perfect match for an already existing program that I would strongly urge you to make use of as you implement this Act. The NSA created the GenCyber ("Generation Cyber") Summer Camp program in 2013 through a partnership with NSF to create a series of summer camps aimed at high school students and high school teachers held on college and university campuses. Summer 2014 was the first year of these camps and there were six very successful camps. DSU held a camp for 172 high school students that were interested in learning more about cybersecurity. 2015 will include 20–25 camps across the Nation and the NSA has a vision to expand GenCyber to be 200+ camps in the coming years in the same way that the "Star Talk" Summer Camps for linguistics has grown and prospered across the Nation (*https://startalk.umd.edu*). Providing support to NSA for GenCyber would be a very wise investment in our children's future as it's critical we continue to get this age group interested in cybersecurity and GenCyber is already two years down this path. Supporting NSA's GenCyber will support not the NSA's goals for this project, but also the GenCyber institutions that are holding camps, and the thousands of high school students that will soon be taking part in these summer experiences. GenCyber has the real potential to change how and when high school students are exposed to cybersecurity education, which is critical as we try to fill the pipeline of exceptional cybersecurity talent.

While there will certainly be new programs and partners involved with the implementation of the Act, it is critical that we look to our trusted partners, as you already done with NSF–SFS CyberCorps, that we know will do a tremendous job and deserve additional support to continue the necessary work in cybersecurity education. The NSA's Center of Academic Excellence in Cyber Operations and GenCyber Summer Camp programs are exactly the type of cybersecurity education partners that deserve direct support as this Act is implemented.

I welcome the chance to provide additional guidance and feedback on S.1353 as it has the potential to help mature cybersecurity education a great deal across the Nation.

———

INTEL CORPORATION
Washington, DC, February 18, 2014

Hon. JOHN THUNE,
Chairman,
United States Senate ,
Committee on Commerce, Science, and
  Transportation,
Washington, DC.

Hon. BILL NELSON,
Ranking Member,
United States Senate,
Committee on Commerce, Science, and
  Transportation,
Washington, DC.

RE: SENATE COMMERCE, SCIENCE, AND TRANSPORTATION COMMITTEE HEARING, "BUILDING A MORE SECURE CYBER FUTURE: EXAMINING PRIVATE SECTOR EXPERIENCE WITH THE NIST FRAMEWORK"

Dear Chairman Thune and Ranking Member Nelson:

Intel Corporation commends you for holding a full committee hearing on February 4, 2015, "Building a More Secure Cyber Future: Examining Private Sector Experience with the NIST Framework," and we thank you for the opportunity to submit written testimony for the record.

We appreciate the Committee's attention to cybersecurity—advancing cybersecurity across the global digital infrastructure has long been a priority for Intel as well. Indeed, security, along with power-efficient performance and connectivity, comprise the three computing pillars around which Intel concentrates our innovation efforts, and Intel has long shared the sentiment that we cannot delay in collectively addressing the evolving cybersecurity threats facing us all. Our commitment to cybersecurity has extended to the Framework for Improving Critical Infrastructure Cybersecurity (the "Framework"), from its inception through its early implementation. President Obama issued Executive Order 13636—Improving Critical Infrastructure Cybersecurity, in February 2013, and over the ensuing year Intel collaborated with government and industry stakeholders to develop the Framework. The first version of the Framework was delivered on February 12, 2014, and soon thereafter Intel launched a pilot project to test the Framework's use at Intel.

Intel's pilot project assessed cybersecurity risk for our Office and Enterprise infrastructure, and demonstrated that the Framework provided clear benefit to Intel. We focused on developing a use case that would create a common language and encourage the use of the Framework as a process and risk management tool, rather than as a set of static compliance requirements. Our early experience with the Framework helped us harmonize our risk management technologies and language, improve our visibility into Intel's risk landscape, inform risk tolerance discussions across our company, and enhance our ability to set security priorities, develop budgets, and deploy security solutions. The pilot resulted in a set of reusable tools and best practices for utilizing the Framework to assess infrastructure risk; we plan to use these tools and best practices to expand Intel's use of the Framework. It is our hope that other organizations follow the path we forged in demonstrating the value of the Framework when it is put in action, by developing their own Framework use cases and driving adoption of the Framework. A detailed account of our pilot project and the benefits we derived from using the Framework is contained in the attached white paper, *The Cybersecurity Framework in Action: An Intel Use Case,* which we respectfully attach for the record.

Thank you again for devoting your Committee's resources to addressing our cybersecurity challenges, and for providing oversight over the Framework. The Framework embodies a longstanding pillar of Intel's cybersecurity strategy: supporting collaboration between government, industry, and non-governmental organization stakeholders to improve cybersecurity in a way that promotes innovation, protects citizens' privacy and civil liberties, and preserves the promise of the Internet as a driver of global economic development and social interaction. We look forward to collaborating with the Committee to achieve our mutual goals moving forward. For more information, please contact John Miller.

Best regards,

PETER M. CLEVELAND,
Vice President,
Global Public Policy Group.

Brief

Cybersecurity Framework
Risk Management

A Cybersecurity Framework Use Case – Intel Corporation

A pilot project reveals key learnings.

By focusing on risk management instead of compliance, the Cybersecurity Framework has the potential to transform cybersecurity on a global scale.

Introduction

Security has long been an Intel priority. Security along with power-efficient performance and connectivity comprise the three computing pillars around which Intel concentrates its innovation efforts. In early 2014, Intel formed the Intel Security Group, a new business unit to further the security pillar. This business unit combines our subsidiary McAfee with all other security resources within Intel, forming a single organization focused on accelerating ubiquitous protection against security risks for people, businesses, and governments worldwide.

Intel has long shared the sentiment with the U.S. and global governments that we cannot delay in collectively addressing the evolving cybersecurity threats that face us all, and Intel and Intel Security will continue to lead efforts to improve cybersecurity across the compute continuum. One way we have demonstrated such leadership is by investing billions of dollars over the last decade to develop software, hardware, services, and integrated solutions to advance cybersecurity across the global digital infrastructure. We also work collaboratively with government, industry, and non-governmental organization stakeholders to improve cybersecurity in a way that promotes innovation, protects citizens' privacy and civil liberties, and preserves the promise of the Internet as a driver of global economic development and social interaction.

Our support for the Cybersecurity Framework (hereafter referred to as the Framework), created as part of U.S. Executive Order 13636, is grounded not only in our prioritization of security but also on thought and operational leadership. The Framework was developed through a process of coordination and collaboration between private industry and public enabling organizations. Through frequent dialogue and collaboration with the National Institute of Standards and Technology (NIST) during the implementation phase, we have devised and implemented an internal risk and management use case for the Framework. We conducted a pilot project to develop this use case.

Cybersecurity Framework Terminology

Core. A set of cybersecurity activities and references that is common across critical infrastructure sectors and organized around particular outcomes. The Framework Core comprises four types of elements: Functions, Categories, Subcategories, and Informative References.

Functions. One of the main components of the Framework, Functions provide the highest level of structure for organizing basic cybersecurity activities into

Categories and Subcategories. The five Functions are Identify, Protect, Detect, Respond, and Recover.

Categories. The subdivision of a Function into groups of cybersecurity outcomes, closely tied to programmatic needs and particular activities. Examples of Categories include Asset Management, Access Control, and Detection Processes.

Subcategories. The subdivision of a Category into specific outcomes of technical and management activities. Examples of Subcategories include External information systems are cataloged, Data-at-rest is protected, and Notifications from detection systems are investigated.

Tiers. The Framework Implementation Tiers ("Tiers") provide context on how an organization views cybersecurity risk and the processes in place to manage that risk. The Tiers range from Partial (Tier 1) to Adaptive (Tier 4) and describe an increasing degree of rigor and sophistication in cybersecurity risk management practices and the extent to which cybersecurity risk management is informed by business needs and integrated into an organization's overall risk management practices.

Profiles. A representation of the outcomes that a particular system or organization has selected from the Framework Categories and Subcategories. Profiles can be used to identify opportunities for improving cybersecurity posture by comparing a current profile (the "as is" state) with a target profile (the "to be" state).

For a more comprehensive glossary of terms, refer to the Cybersecurity Framework document.
www.nist.gov/cyberframework/upload/cybersecurity-framework-021214.pdf

The Pilot in Context

We are at the preliminary stages of understanding the Framework. As the development of the Framework was nearing its completion, former NIST Director Pat Gallagher said we were "at the end of the beginning." Dr. Gallagher's words hold true today, less than a year since Framework 1.0 was released. Nonetheless, as an organization currently using the Framework, we will continue to evolve and use the Framework on an ongoing basis.

> We are at the preliminary stages of understanding the Framework.

By implementing the Framework, we anticipate that Intel will achieve the following benefits:

- Harmonization of risk management methodologies, technologies, and language across the enterprise
- Improved visibility into Intel's risk landscape, helping identify both strengths and opportunities to improve
- Better-informed risk tolerance discussions
- Ability to better set security priorities, develop capital and operational expenditure budgets, and identify potential security solutions and practices

Throughout the development process, Intel actively supported the emergence of the Framework from its initial public comment phase by participating in the Framework development workshops and by providing comments to the draft documents that NIST published. Intel believes that the strength of the Framework lies in its accessibility and flexibility; we are committed to proactively developing a Framework use case to both demonstrate industry leadership and provide key learnings to drive the evolution of the Framework. We believe the Framework's evolution is and will continue to be an industry-led effort as we move forward.

Utilizing the Cybersecurity Framework at Intel

From the early days of development, the Intel team responsible for engaging with the Framework planned to conduct a pilot project to test its use at Intel. Once the 1.0 version of the Framework was released and we knew the final configuration, we looked for a business unit to partner with for the pilot. Because we were in new territory, we sought a mature business unit with a robust cybersecurity program and with a large range of products and services we could use to test some of the Framework's limits. Intel IT met all these requirements, making it the obvious choice.

Intel IT is much more than a service organization. As an integral part of the Intel business, it delivers value by offering solutions to other business units that drive other products. Intel IT's cybersecurity program has a large number of cybersecurity experts, all of whom could easily provide independent assessment and evaluation under the Framework with minimal training. Intel IT also uses a mature model of cyber functions within the enterprise (the *DOMES* model detailed in the Design section) that enabled us to further simplify the pilot.

We have recently completed the pilot project, which clearly demonstrated the value of the Framework. We plan to apply what we learned during the pilot to expanding Intel's use of the Framework. Most importantly, we verified that by focusing on risk management rather than compliance, the Framework has the potential to transform cybersecurity on a global scale and accelerate cybersecurity across the compute continuum.

Methodology

Intel uses different risk management tools in different situations, depending on the environment being managed and the type and scope of the risks. We consider the Framework to be a top-level security management tool that helps assess cybersecurity risk across the enterprise. Intel's approach was to conduct the pilot using the Framework to create an enterprise-level risk heat map that could be used to do the following:

- Set risk tolerance baselines

- Identify areas that need more detailed or technical assessments

- Identify areas of overinvestment and underinvestment

- Assist in risk prioritization

Design

For assessment purposes, Intel divides its compute infrastructure into five critical business functions: *Design, Office, Manufacturing, Enterprise*, and *Services (DOMES)*. For the pilot project, we used the Framework to perform an initial high-level risk assessment on only the *Office* and *Enterprise* environments, rather than attempt to apply the Framework across the entire computing domain. Because *Office* and *Enterprise* are similar environments from a risk management perspective, the subject matter experts (SMEs) involved in the Framework risk assessment pilot were essentially the same people. Also, the *Office* and *Enterprise* environments most closely match the existing Framework Categories (see the Cybersecurity Framework Terminology sidebar), while we believe the other business functions, such as *Manufacturing* and *Design*, may require more customization of the Framework Categories.

The pilot project involved three main groups of people:

- The Core Group, comprising 8 to 10 senior security SMEs and mid-to-senior-level security capability or program managers, who set target scores, validated Categories, developed Subcategories, and performed an initial risk assessment and scoring.

- Individual security SMEs, who scored the risk areas.

- Stakeholders and decision makers, who approved target scores, reviewed assessment results, and set risk tolerance levels.

The activities of these groups are described in more detail in the Implementing the Pilot Project section.

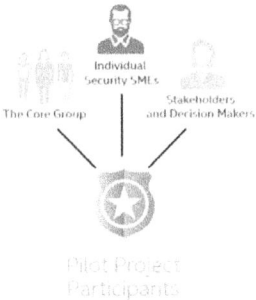

Individual
Security SMEs

The Core Group

Stakeholders
and Decision Makers

Pilot Project
Participants

Goals

We established the following goals for the pilot Framework project, which sought to assess cybersecurity risk for the Office and Enterprise infrastructure:

- Establish organizational alignment on risk tolerance objectives.

- Inform the budget planning and prioritization processes.

- Communicate an aligned cybersecurity risk picture to senior leadership.

- Create a set of reusable tools and best practices for utilizing the Framework to assess infrastructure risk.

Early in the planning, we believed the Framework could transform a discussion about risk tolerance objectives from implicit to explicit. Today it is not unusual for an organization to have a disconnect between the C-level and the technical implementation staff level concerning risk tolerance, and often the organization is unaware of this problem. With a definitive, universal understanding of what an organization's governance considers an acceptable level of risk, the organization can now compare current and target scores to determine where improvements may be made.

Implementing the Pilot Project

During the implementation of the pilot project, we did not treat the Framework as a recipe book, but rather as the framework that it is. As such, we felt empowered to tailor it to meet our business needs. We believe that organizations implementing the Framework should also consider tailoring it to fit their individual business processes and priorities, to maximize the benefits they can gain.

We customized the Framework in the following areas:

- **Tier definitions.** We augmented the generic Tier definitions listed in the Framework to provide more concrete guidance to our assessors, as applicable to our particular environment.

  We started with the traditional security triad of People, Processes, and Technology, and mapped the Framework definitions into that structure. We then added a new element, Ecosystem, which we believe is equally essential to a modern corporate security program. Important organizational and governance issues, not included in the core model, are now included in this new element.

  Our modifications remained aligned to the Framework Tiers' graduated maturity scale and intent. Table 1 lists our customized Tier definitions.

- **Categories.** In the Detect Function, we added a fourth Category, Threat Intelligence, because it is an important part of Intel's security processes. We expect additional Categories to emerge as we apply the Framework to Intel's *Design*, *Manufacturing*, and *Services* environments.

- **Subcategories.** After much consideration, we decided not to use most of the Subcategories as defined by the Framework. While the supplied Subcategories are appropriate for most environments, we created our own Subcategories to better reflect how Intel manages each Category. For example, in Asset Management we created the Subcategories of Information, Client, Server, Network, People, and Virtual, which align with the scheme Intel IT Security uses to manage assets. In addition, we found Subcategories were necessary to our assessment pilot only if that level of granularity helped inform a business decision. For example, if the Asset Management Category received a low score, the Subcategories could help identify the specific aspects needing improvement.

Table 1. Customized Tier Definitions

FOCUS AREA	TIER 1 PARTIAL	TIER 2 RISK INFORMED	TIER 3 REPEATABLE	TIER 4 ADAPTIVE
People	• Cybersecurity professionals (staff) and the general employee population have had little to no cybersecurity-related training. • The staff has a limited or nonexistent training pipeline. • Security awareness is limited. • Employees have little or no awareness of company security resources and escalation paths.	• The staff and employees have received cybersecurity-related training. • The staff has a training pipeline. • There is an awareness of cybersecurity risk at the organizational level. • Employees have a general awareness of security and company security resources and escalation paths.	• The staff possesses the knowledge and skills to perform their appointed roles and responsibilities. • Employees should receive regular cybersecurity-related training and briefings. • The staff has a robust training pipeline, including internal and external security conferences or training opportunities. • Organization and business units have a security champion or dedicated security staff.	• The staff's knowledge and skills are regularly reviewed for currency and applicability and new skills, and knowledge needs are identified and addressed. • Employees receive regular cybersecurity-related training and briefings on relevant and emerging security topics. • The staff has a robust training pipeline and routinely attend internal and external security conferences or training opportunities.

Process	• A risk management process has not been formalized; risks are managed in a reactive, ad hoc manner. • Business decisions and prioritization are not factored into risk and threat assessments. • Risk and threat information is not communicated to internal stakeholders.	• Prioritization of cybersecurity activities is informed by organizational risk objectives, the threat environment, or mission requirements. • Risk-informed, management-approved processes and procedures are defined and implemented, and the staff has adequate resources to perform its cybersecurity duties. • Cybersecurity information is shared within the organization on an informal basis. • Management has approved the risk management practices, but these practices may not have been established as organizational-wide policy.	• Organizational cybersecurity practices are regularly updated based on the application of risk management processes to changes in business or mission requirements and a changing threat and technology landscape. • Consistent risk management practices are formally approved and expressed as policy, and there is an organization-wide approach to manage cybersecurity risk. • Risk-informed policies, processes, and procedures are defined, implemented as intended, and reviewed.	• Cybersecurity risk management is an integral part of the organizational culture. • The organization actively adapts to a changing cybersecurity landscape, evolving and sophisticated threats, predictive indicators, and lessons learned from previous events in a timely manner. • The organization continually incorporates advanced cybersecurity technologies and practices. • There is an organization-wide approach to managing cybersecurity risk that uses risk-informed policies, processes, and procedures.
Technology	• Tools to help manage cybersecurity risk are not deployed, not supported, or insufficient to address risks. • Tools may be in place but are not adequately tuned or maintained. • Technology deployed lags current threats. • Tool deployment may not adequately cover risk areas.	• Tools are deployed and supported to address identified risks. • The tools in deployment are tuned and maintained when resources are available. • The technology deployed, for the most part, keeps pace with current threats. • Tool coverage of the risk area is complete when deployed.	• Metrics are used to evaluate the usefulness and effectiveness of the deployed tools. • The tools in deployment are routinely tuned and maintained. • The technology deployed keeps pace with current and emerging threats. • Tool coverage of the risk area is complete and updated as changes are recognized.	• The tools deployed in the environment are regularly reviewed for effectiveness and coverage against changes in the threat environment and internal ecosystem. • The tools and technology deployed anticipate emerging threats.
Ecosystem	• The organization does not understand its role in the larger ecosystem or act accordingly. • The organization does not have processes in place to participate in or collaborate with external organizations on cybersecurity issues.	• The organization knows its role in the larger ecosystem but has not formalized its capabilities to interact and share information externally. • The organization may participate in or collaborate with external organizations on cybersecurity issues on an ad hoc basis.	• The organization understands its ecosystem dependencies and partners and can act accordingly when it receives information from these partners.	• The organization manages risk and actively shares information with partners to ensure that accurate, current information improves ecosystem cybersecurity before events occur.

Project Phases

Our pilot project consisted of four phases: set target scores, assess our current status, analyze the results of that assessment, and communicate those results to managers and senior leadership. An organized, phased approach enabled us to successfully implement the Framework in our *Office* and *Enterprise* environments.

We completed the project in about seven months.

- **Phase 1 – Set target scores.** The Core Group held a one-day, face-to-face session and a half-day virtual session during which the following actions took place:

  - Agreed on methodology and maturity descriptions

  - Validated Functions and Categories and defined new Subcategories aligned to Intel's capabilities, programs, and processes

  - Assigned target scores by Function and Category

  - Assessed current status and scored Functions and Categories

As a result of this initial phase we were able to validate that our approach aligned with Intel's existing risk management methodologies and could be a meaningful tool for prioritization and risk tolerance decisions. Our chief information security officer (CISO) and other key stakeholders also validated our target scores, further raising our confidence that we had set them accurately.

- **Phase 2 – Assess current status.** We identified senior SME scorers to conduct an independent risk assessment based on the Framework. Using learnings from our Core Group sessions, we developed individual scoring tools and provided training through virtual one-hour sessions (see Training Topics for more information). Once trained, the SMEs individually scored the Categories and noted specific Subcategories where opportunities to improve existed.

  By design, participants were not aware of the target scores that the Core Group set. The total time that each SME used for the assessment was 2 to 3 hours, which included training, using the self-scoring tool, and participating in a validation of the aggregated scores.

- **Phase 3 – Analyze results.** We analyzed the individual SME scores and compared them to the Core Group scores and the target scores (see Figure 1). Significant differences between Core Group and individual SME scores can identify visibility issues, either by the individual SME or the Core Group.

  Using a heat map format to identify score differences greater than one, we examined areas of concern at the Subcategory level to further identify specific areas for improvement.

- **Phase 4 – Communicate results.** We reviewed our findings and recommendations with the CISO and staff. A key component of this phase was to revalidate target scores with the CISO and key stakeholders, in the context of the assessed scores. This process fostered a dialogue and helped us agree on risk tolerance and prioritization.

  We also informed the capability and process owners who were impacted by the results of our discussion. Conveying this information helped us prioritize the key issues in the budgeting and planning cycles and examine where additional, more granular risk assessments should be prioritized.

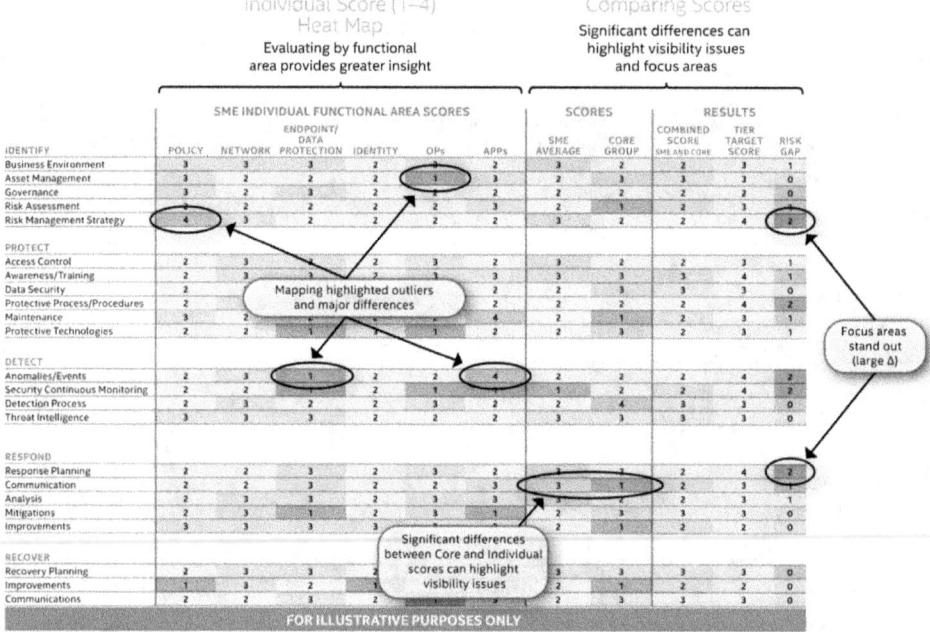

Figure 1. A heat map resulting from charting individual and group scores and their comparisons. *Note: The scores given are examples and not the actual scores.*

Training Topics

We provided training to the SMEs who would be performing the individual scoring. We also trained facilitators who will be able to conduct future risk assessment sessions with Core Group members and SMEs to set the target score and perform the Tier target scoring.

- **SME training.** Topics included a brief history of the Framework and why Intel is implementing it, an explanation of how the assessment fits within Intel's decision making process, and a use case example. These one-hour training sessions were delivered virtually and included a question-and-answer period at the end.

- **Facilitator training.** Topics included guidance on the customized Tier maturity descriptions, the difference between the target and assessed scores, and how the prioritization/risk tolerance discussion is handled. We stressed the importance of adhering to the process flow and repeating the process year over year.

Results and Benefits

One of the most important and valuable benefits of the Framework pilot project was the internal discussions it helped foster. Conversations about defining the organization's Profile to determine the various levels of risk the organization is willing to accept are extremely valuable in aligning and prioritizing an organization's cybersecurity risk management activities. The target score versus assessed score discussions were especially instructive, as they enabled participants to discuss and compare risks across domains in a common language and on common ground. They also helped facilitate agreement between stakeholders and leadership on risk tolerance and other strategic risk management issues, understandings which in turn can guide the organization in security project prioritization and funding.

One of the most important outcomes of our pilot was proving the value of establishing an organization-specific Profile through internal dialogue based on the threats, vulnerabilities, and impacts the organization faces. Because these security aspects are best understood by an organization going through this process itself, we believe that creating a tailored Tiers Profile will provide the most value for organizations.

We also gained the following benefits:

- The Framework pilot project was effective in improving alignment to a common risk management methodology and language across internal stakeholder communities.

- When we started to define our own Subcategories, we again found value in the dialogue, which resulted in improved cross-team alignment on the processes and capabilities that comprised a Category. In addition, the Subcategories specific to Intel enabled SMEs and stakeholders to better understand the Categories. Finally, by aligning the Subcategories to our capabilities, we can more easily see where more detailed assessment is needed.

- Mapping assessments of common Core items by SMEs in a single risk heat map enabled quick identification of outliers, significant variances, and visibility issues. Highlighting these issues led to additional discussion and assessment, allowing us to further improve visibility into our risk landscape.

  By similarly mapping results from across other elements of our infrastructure (*Manufacturing, Design*, and so on) we anticipate being able to visualize certain organizational trends and groupings regarding our risk landscape. Gaining the benefit of these new insights would be more difficult without a unifying mechanism like the Framework.

- The pilot project resulted in developing tools that we can reuse as we expand the Framework's use across Intel. These tools included the following:

  - Risk-scoring worksheet
  - Heat map

○ Customized Tier definitions (People, Process, Technology, Ecosystem)

• The training materials for assessors and facilitators developed during the pilot project can be reused.

We achieved these results with a cost of under 175 FTE (full-time employee) hours. This low cost was due to several factors, including the Framework's alignment to existing industry risk management practices and our own established risk management culture and set of practices across Intel business units.

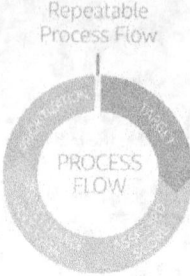

Key Learnings

The following list summarizes the key learnings attained during our pilot project.

• **Start where you are comfortable.** It made the most sense for us to start with the *Office* and *Enterprise* business functions because our IT Security organization had already begun similar efforts that we could leverage as far as management commitment and resources. These existing efforts meant that the *Office* and *Enterprise* risks were fairly well understood, so we could apply the Framework quickly. Also, the existing Framework Categories map well to the *Office* and *Enterprise* environments.

Now that we have proved the validity of the Framework and shown that we can gain value from it, we can scale the application of the Framework to our other *DOMES* functions, such as *Design* and *Manufacturing*.

• **Perform continual iteration with the decision makers throughout the process.** Cyber risk management is not an end result; it is a continual process. Therefore, an ongoing process of iteration and validation results in a ongoing dialogue about risk. This process also results in a more successful Framework implementation, because the SMEs and the decision makers give and receive feedback—better aligning the Framework to the organization's business processes and priorities.

• **Use group collaboration mixed with individual scoring.** We found that the Core Group's initial work, combined with individual SME assessment and scoring, provided more effective results than if we had used just a single approach. For example, the dialogue that occurred between the Core Group members was especially helpful in setting the target scores. In contrast, the individual SME scoring and input proved valuable because it provided a deeper drill down and a SME-specific perspective, such as networking or operations.

• **Tailor the Framework to your business.** We believe that an organization should define a Tiers Profile that best fits that organization's needs. Additionally, adding, changing, or deleting Categories and Subcategories helps the Framework align with an organization's business environment. All of the work that our own team did provided invaluable discussion and insights that we could not have found externally, imported from other sources.

Conclusion

While we are at the preliminary stages of fully understanding the Framework and how it can be deployed across Intel, our early experience with the Framework has proved valuable. Some of the benefits realized through our Framework pilot project in the *Office* and *Enterprise* environments include harmonization of risk management technologies and language across the enterprise; improved visibility into Intel's risk landscape, helping identify both strengths and opportunities to improve; better-informed risk tolerance discussions; and the ability to better set security priorities, develop capital and operational expenditure budgets, and deploy security solutions.

We plan to extend our successful Framework pilot project to other areas of Intel's critical business functions, such as *Design, Manufacturing*, and *Services* over the coming months.[1] As we continue working with the Framework at Intel, we hope to gain a better understanding of Tiers and plan to further explore the use of Categories and Subcategories. As various internal risk management and governance processes start or reach appropriate milestones, we will also introduce Framework concepts and integrate applicable portions into these processes.

We believe that as the Framework matures and evolves it should include the cyber threat intelligence lifecycle. Automated indicator sharing is included in the Framework Roadmap,[2] however, that is just the mechanism by which intelligence can be shared. Cyber threat intelligence is a much broader discipline, essential to a robust cybersecurity risk management program and needs attention in the Framework. Organizations must have a robust understanding of the following cyber threat intelligence aspects to best prepare for and respond to cybersecurity attacks:

- Relevant threat agents and actors
- Threat agents' and actors' tactics, techniques, and procedures
- Incidents and campaigns

Incident handling and vulnerability management are also essential pieces of cybersecurity risk management and warrant consideration for inclusion in future versions of the Framework.

Because we believe other organizations can also benefit from deploying the Framework, Intel and Intel Security are participating in extensive outreach regarding the Framework. This outreach includes meeting with governmental officials, attending conferences, seminars, webinars, and summits, and publishing blogs. Raising awareness and encouraging best practices is an integral and ongoing part of Intel's efforts to foster improvements in global cyber risk management; in our initial experience the Framework has proved a useful tool in furthering these overall efforts.

To read about the Cybersecurity Framework, visit: www.nist.gov/cyberframework

For more information about Intel's technology solutions for federal government, visit: www.intel.com/federal

Follow the conversation: #intelfederal

Authors

Tim Casey
Senior Strategic Risk Analyst, Intel Security Group

Kevin Fiftal
Civilian Director, Intel Americas

Kent Landfield
Director, Standards and Technology Policy, Intel Security Group

John Miller
Director, Cybersecurity Policy & Strategy, Intel Global Public Policy

Dennis Morgan
Chief Security Architect, Intel Information Technology

Brian Willis
Manager, Threat Intelligence and Infrastructure Protection, Intel Security Group

67

Contributors

The authors wish to thank their colleagues who contributed to the pilot process, provided technical content, and reviewed this document. The authors would like to acknowledge Jack Lawson and Amit Agrawal for their valuable assistance throughout the development of this document. Thank you also to Jason Kimrey of Intel for his support and leadership of this project.

1 For more information about how Intel is approaching security in its Manufacturing environment, see "Factory of the Future," 2014. www.mcafee.com/us/resources/white-papers/wp-factory-future.pdf

2 For more information, see the "NIST Roadmap for Improving Critical Infrastructure Cybersecurity," 2014. www.nist.gov/cyberframework/upload/roadmap-021214.pdf

RETAIL INDUSTRY LEADERS ASSOCIATION
Arlington, VA, February 4, 2015

Hon. JOHN THUNE,
Chairman,
Senate Committee on Commerce,
  Science, and Transportation,
United States Senate,
Washington, DC.

Hon. BILL NELSON,
Ranking Member,
Senate Committee on Commerce,
  Science, and Transportation,
United States Senate,
Washington, DC.

Dear Chairman Thune and Ranking Member Nelson:

On behalf of the Retail Industry Leaders Association (RILA), I write to thank you for holding today's hearing entitled, "Building a More Secure Cyber Future: Examining Private Sector Experience with the NIST Framework." Retailers greatly appreciate the Committee's leadership in seeking to find a sensible path to address critical cybersecurity issues.

RILA is the trade association of the world's largest and most innovative retail companies. RILA members include more than 200 retailers, product manufacturers, and service suppliers, which together are responsible for more than $1.5 trillion in annual sales, millions of American jobs and more than 100,000 stores, manufacturing facilities and distribution centers domestically and abroad.

Retailers embrace innovative technology to provide American consumers with unparalleled services and products online, through mobile applications, and in our stores. While technology presents great opportunity, nation states, criminal organizations, and other bad actors also are using it to attack businesses, institutions, and governments. As we have seen, no organization is immune from attacks and no security system is invulnerable. Retailers understand that defense against cyber-attacks must be an ongoing effort, evolving to address the changing nature of the threat. RILA is committed to working with Congress to give government and retailers the tools necessary to thwart this unprecedented attack on the United States (U.S.) economy and bring the fight to cybercriminals around the globe.

As leaders in the retail community, we are taking new and significant steps to enhance cybersecurity throughout the industry. To that end, RILA formed the Retail Cyber Intelligence Sharing Center (R–CISC) in 2014 in partnership with America's most recognized retailers. The Center has opened a steady flow of information sharing between retailers, law enforcement and other relevant stakeholders. These efforts already have helped prevent data breaches, protected millions of American customers and saved retailers millions of dollars. The R–CISC is open to all retailers regardless of their membership in RILA.

For years, RILA members have been developing and deploying new technologies to achieve pioneering levels of security and service. The cyber-attacks that our industry faces change every day and our members are building layered and resilient systems to meet these threats. Key to this effort is the ability to design systems to meet actual threats rather than potentially outdated cybersecurity standards that may be enshrined in law. That is why development of any technical cybersecurity standards beyond a mandate for reasonable security must be voluntary and industry-led such as the standards embodied in the National Institute of Standards and Technology Cybersecurity Framework. RILA members using the Framework have found it to be a helpful tool in evaluating their cybersecurity posture and support the continued use of voluntary, industry-led processes as a key method of addressing dynamic technology challenges.

One area of cybersecurity that needs immediate attention is payment card technology. RILA members have long supported the adoption of stronger debit and credit card security protections. The woefully outdated magnetic stripe technology used on cards today is the chief vulnerability in the payments ecosystem. This 1960s era technology allows cyber criminals to create counterfeit cards and commit fraud with ease. Retailers continue to press banks and card networks to provide U.S. consumers with the same Chip and PIN technology that has proven to dramatically reduce fraud when it has been deployed elsewhere around the world. According to the Federal Reserve, PINs on debit cards make them 700 percent more secure than transactions authorized by signature.[1]

Increasing cyber threat information sharing is also vital to defeating sophisticated and coordinated cyber actors. RILA strongly supports cybersecurity information sharing legislation that provides liability protections for participating organizations. Legislation also should increase funding for government sponsored research into

---

[1] Federal Reserve, "2011 Interchange Fee Revenue, Covers Issuer Costs, and Covered Issuer and Merchant Fraud Losses Related to Debit Card Transactions," (March 5, 2013).

next generation security controls and enhance law enforcement capabilities to investigate and prosecute criminals internationally. The cyber-attacks faced by every sector of our economy constitute a grave national security threat that should be addressed from all angles.

RILA thanks the Committee for holding this important hearing to look into the positive private sector experience with the NIST Cybersecurity Framework, cyber information sharing legislation, and cybersecurity more broadly. We look forward to working with you on these vital issues. Should you have any additional questions regarding this matter, please feel free to contact Nicholas Ahrens, Vice President, Privacy and Cybersecurity.

Sincerely,

JENNIFER M. SAFAVIAN,
Executive Vice President, Government Affairs.

PREPARED STATEMENT OF INDEPENDENT COMMUNITY BANKERS OF AMERICA (ICBA)

CYBERSECURITY: THE COMMUNITY BANK PERSPECTIVE

On behalf of the more than 6,500 community banks represented by ICBA, thank you for convening today's hearing on "Building a More Secure Cyber Future: Examining Private Sector Experience with the NIST Framework." The financial services industry and community banks are typically on the front lines of defending against cybersecurity threats and take their role in securing data and personal information very seriously. ICBA is pleased to take this opportunity to submit the following statement for the record which sets forth the community bank perspective on cybersecurity and the National Institute for Standards and Technology (NIST) framework.

All Critical Infrastructure Sectors Must Be Covered and Existing Mandates Must Be Recognized. ICBA supports the 2013 Executive Order and the NIST framework implementing it because they create a baseline to reduce cyber risk to all critical infrastructure sectors. This is a critical test for any new legislation, frameworks, or standards in the area of data security: It should extend comparable standards to all critical infrastructure sectors, including the commercial facilities sector which incorporates the retail industry and other potentially vulnerable entities. Financial institutions have long been subject to rigorous and effective data security protocols established by the Gramm-Leach-Bliley Act. Any new data security mandates must recognize the existing standards and practices community banks observe to protect the confidentiality and integrity of customer personal data as well as to mitigate cyber threats.

Threat Information Sharing is Critical. ICBA supports the sharing of advanced threat and attack data between Federal agencies and the appropriate financial sector participants, including community banks. Community banks rely on this critical information to help them manage their cyber threats and protect their systems. ICBA supports community banks' involvement with services such as the Financial Services Information Sharing and Analysis Center (FS–ISAC). The FS–ISAC is a non-profit, information-sharing forum established by financial services industry participants to facilitate the public and private sectors' sharing of physical and cybersecurity threat and vulnerability information. ICBA also supports FS–ISAC efforts to take complex threat information across communities, people and devices and analyze, prioritize, and route it to users in real-time as long as those efforts incorporate community banks and such advancements are cost effective to community banks.

Regulators Should Recognize Third Party Risk. Community banks significantly rely on third parties to support their systems and business activities. While community banks are diligent in their management of third parties, mitigating sophisticated cyber threats to these third parties, especially when they have connections to other institutions and servicers, can be challenging. Regulators must be aware of the significant interconnectivity of these third parties and must collaborate with them to mitigate this risk. This can be done by agencies evaluating the concentration risks of service providers to financial institutions, and broadening supervision of technology service providers to include more core, IT service providers by expanding the Multi-Regional Data Processing Servicer Program (MDPS) to include such providers.

Properly Aligned Incentives Will Enhance Data Security and Cybersecurity. When an entity's systems are breached, it is critical that the party that incurs the breach, whether it be a retailer, financial institution, data processor or other entity, bear responsibility for the related fraud losses and costs of mitigation. Allocating financial responsibility with the party that incurs the breach will provide a strong incentive for all parties to effectively secure data.

Additionally, aligning incentives to maximize data security and cybersecurity by all parties that process and/or store consumer data will make the payments system stronger over time.

Thank you again for convening today's hearing. ICBA looks forward to working with the Senate Committee on Commerce, Science, and Transportation to improve cybersecurity.

———

RESPONSE TO WRITTEN QUESTIONS SUBMITTED BY HON. JOHN THUNE TO
DR. CHARLES H. ROMINE

Question 1. Dr. Romine, in follow up to my question at the hearing, please provide for the record examples of products and services that the private sector is developing to support use of the Framework.

Answer. A variety of products and services have been developed by the private sector, including, but not limited to, implementation guides, mappings to the Framework, case studies, educational materials, example profiles, and other document templates. Recently, NIST added an "Industry Resources" link to the Cybersecurity Framework website (*www.nist.gov/cyberframework*) which is a non-exhaustive list of these resources to share for broader use.

It is important to note that in doing this certain commercial entities, equipment, or materials may be identified in this Website or linked websites in order to support Framework understanding and use. Such identification is not intended to imply recommendation or endorsement by NIST, nor is it intended to imply that the entities, materials, or equipment are necessarily the best available for the purpose.

Question 2. In response to my question, you testified briefly regarding the feedback NIST has received in its draft Guide to Cyber Threat Information Sharing. NIST also has identified automated indicator sharing as one of the areas for development, alignment, and collaboration in its Roadmap for Improving Critical Infrastructure Cybersecurity released on February 12, 2014. Would you please elaborate on NIST's work to develop technical standards for information sharing, including machine-to-machine sharing, for use in both the public and private sectors?

Answer. While the NIST draft Special Publication 800–150, *Guide to Cyber Threat Information Sharing,* provides high-level guidance on how to form, join, and effectively participate in information sharing communities, NIST has also participated in, and led significant initiatives to develop technical standards for information sharing. NIST's Security Content Automation Protocol (SCAP) specifications provide low-level technical guidance in support of automated information exchange. SCAP is a suite of interoperable open technical specifications, developed through ongoing public-private collaboration, that enable automated, machine-to-machine exchange of information. SCAP-validated tools can be used to evaluate the security posture of an IT system. SCAP is used to describe known security vulnerabilities, identify configuration issues, and to collect system artifacts that can attest to the system's current security state and to develop and publish indicators.

In addition to our role in the development of the SCAP specifications, NIST operates the National Vulnerability Database (NVD), the U.S. government repository of SCAP content. The NVD repository includes information regarding over 68,000 known software flaws, 281 security checklists that provide security configuration guidance for operating systems and applications, and over 101,000 product names and identifiers. The NVD-hosted SCAP content and resources are widely used by both public and private sector organizations, including many commercial anti-virus software developers.

NIST continues to engage with both the private sector and Federal departments and agencies to help develop and refine technical specifications that enable the near-real-time exchange of cyber threat indicators. Through its participation in consensus-driven standards development efforts, such as the International Organization for Standardization's (ISO) Joint Technical Committee 1 (JTC1), NIST is able to help advance the development of technical specifications that enable the creation, use, and automated exchange of indicator data.

Question 3. In addition to automated indicator sharing, NIST identified a number of additional areas for development, alignment, and collaboration in its Roadmap for Improving Critical Infrastructure Cybersecurity, released on February 12, 2014. Subsequently, on December 5, 2014, NIST released an update reflecting the responses and feedback received in response to its August 26, 2014, Request for Information. Please provide an update on NIST's role, current status, and path forward to address each of the following areas: authentication, conformity assessment, cybersecurity workforce, data analytics, Federal agency cybersecurity alignment, supply chain risk management, and technical privacy standards.

Answer. NIST's role in cybersecurity is to develop information security standards, guidelines, tests, and metrics to protect non-national security Federal information, systems, and services against threats impacting their confidentiality, integrity and availability, by conducting research that generates the data needed to support these tools. As part of this mission, NIST facilitates and plays an active role in the development of voluntary, industry-led cybersecurity standards and best practices. NIST accomplishes its mission in cybersecurity through collaborative partnerships with our customers and stakeholders in industry, government, academia, standards organizations and international partners.

The Roadmap for Improving Critical Infrastructure Cybersecurity highlighted several areas identified by stakeholders that require continued focus; they are important but evolving areas that have yet to be developed or need further research and understanding. While tools, methodologies, and standards exist for some of the areas, they need to become more mature, available, and widely adopted. NIST continues to work with stakeholders in each of these areas to identify primary challenges, solicit input to address those identified needs, and collaboratively develop and execute action plans for addressing them. NIST is actively engaging with diverse stakeholders through existing programs, including the National Strategy for Trusted Identities in Cyberspace (NSTIC) and the National Initiative for Cybersecurity Education (NICE), to identify primary challenges, solicit input, and develop and execute plans to address those identified needs in each of the areas identified in the roadmap.

Question 4. The U.S. Chamber of Commerce has noted that standards are most effective when developed and recognized globally, which can help to prevent the burden of multiple, conflicting jurisdictional requirements. The Cybersecurity Enhancement Act (Public Law 113–274) recognized NIST's convening role in international standards development and required NIST to consult with foreign governments and international organizations to support the Framework development process. Please elaborate on the importance of global alignment in cybersecurity and how NIST has worked with international organizations to promote the Framework and the public-private partnership model overseas.

Answer. Pursuant to U.S. law and Administration policy, Federal agencies are required to use voluntary consensus standards in their procurement and regulatory activities, except where inconsistent with law or otherwise impractical. The U.S. consensus standardization community is comprised mostly of non-governmental standards developers. These groups are primarily shaped by extensive industry participation and are market driven. U.S. government participation is motivated by the need to achieve cost-efficient, timely and effective solutions to regulatory, procurement and policy objectives. These diverse motivations are mutually beneficial.

Meanwhile, many governments are proposing and enacting strategies, policies, laws, and regulations covering information technology for critical infrastructure. Because many organizations and most sectors operate globally or rely on the global digital infrastructure, these requirements are affecting, or may affect, how organizations operate, conduct business, and develop new products and services. Diverse or specialized requirements that vary by country or region, can impede interoperability, result in duplication, harm cybersecurity, and hinder innovation. In turn, this can significantly reduce the availability and use of innovative technologies to critical infrastructures in all industries and hamper the ability of organizations to operate globally and to effectively manage new and evolving risks.

Because the Framework references globally accepted standards, guidelines and practice, organizations domiciled inside and outside of the United States can use the Framework to efficiently operate globally and manage new and evolving risks.

During the development of the Framework and since its completion, NIST has engaged with foreign governments and private sector entities to explain the Framework and seek alignment of approaches when possible; worked with industry stakeholders to support their international engagement; and exchanged information with standards developing organizations, and the public and private sectors to ensure the Cybersecurity Framework remains aligned and compatible with existing and developing standards and practices.

Question 5. How has NIST worked with insurance companies in particular in developing the Framework? How do insurance policies provide an incentive for companies to increase their cybersecurity?

Answer. During the development of the Framework, NIST sought the participation of insurance companies, given their extensive knowledge of the effectiveness of specific cybersecurity practices and their ability to help evaluate specific proposed elements from this perspective. This collaboration included a panel at the 4th Cybersecurity Framework Workshop in Dallas, Texas, where panelists from AIG, ACE USA, Willis, and Lockton answered questions from the audience, and discussed the current state of the cybersecurity insurance market, how the Cybersecurity Framework could help insurance carriers grow the first-party market and be incorporated into underwriting/brokering processes, and anticipated challenges that may arise. According to the Department of Homeland Security—who NIST has partnered with on projects relating to cybersecurity insurance industry: "A robust cybersecurity insurance market could help reduce the number of successful cyber attacks by: (1) promoting the adoption of preventative measures in return for more coverage; and (2) encouraging the implementation of best practices by basing premiums on an insured's level of self-protection."[1]

As industry continues to use the Framework, and insurance companies leverage the Framework to provide policies and services, NIST will continue to work with them to understand their specific implementations and how it could inform future work.

———

RESPONSE TO WRITTEN QUESTION SUBMITTED BY HON. ROY BLUNT TO DR. CHARLES H. ROMINE

Question. The Framework itself is voluntary and based upon a risk management model, as opposed to compliance with rote standards. Wouldn't the concept of a mandatory survey be counter to the voluntary approach adopted by NIST, and could it impact the use of the Framework if private sector owners and operators of critical infrastructure view using the Framework as being linked to new reporting requirements? Please provide your perspective on the mandatory survey proposal.

Answer. NIST believes that a mandatory survey would be premature and will not provide meaningful results to help determine the adoption of the Framework. Adding a mandatory reporting requirement on top of a voluntary Framework could create confusion about the intent of the Executive Order and lead to less participation and use of the Framework, as well as reduce trust in NIST's consensus development process adversely affecting future participation.

After some time has passed, measurement of use and effectiveness of the Framework is an element of NIST's plans. Costs (including burden on companies) and benefits of doing that as well as alternative options would be considered at that time. Measurement should also include how products and services—and the overall market forces—are supporting use of the Framework, and where legislative changes may assist with use.

Based on feedback from the private sector, the immediate focus of the Administration is on raising awareness about the value of the voluntary Framework in addressing and reducing risk, and encouraging its use. NIST continues to hear from the private sector—including our most recent discussions with leaders across many sectors—that raising awareness and stimulating use are the essential first steps on the path to achieving effectiveness.

NIST believes that this is the pathway to effectiveness. Concerns about cybersecurity and risk need to be integrated into each organization's approach for doing business. There is no single, definitive and universal end point for improving quality or cybersecurity. NIST is asking organizations to do a serious evaluation of their current cybersecurity practices and develop plans to improve their capabilities through use of the Framework—a process that will take time.

NIST is also seeing a range of products and services being developed or modified to assist organizations use the Cybersecurity Framework. The Administration is also working to ensure that this approach can scale globally—as NIST sees that alignment it's likely to also see increased use of the Framework for companies with international business.

The voluntary nature of the framework in enabling a larger number of stakeholders to use the underlying practices—choosing a subset for a mandatory survey might create an impression that only this subset should use the Framework. The private sector voluntarily participated in the Framework development process and NIST has found that organizations are willing to discuss how they are using or intend to use the Framework. NIST will work with DHS on their sector-wide assessments, monitor surveys that private sector organizations conduct, and will continue to receive information through workshops, meetings, and potentially future Requests for Information. Much of this will be geared to gathering information on how to improve future versions of the Framework.

---

[1] *http://www.dhs.gov/publication/cybersecurity-insurance*

RESPONSE TO WRITTEN QUESTIONS SUBMITTED BY HON. JOHN THUNE TO
ANN M. BEAUCHESNE

Question 1. In August 2013, the Department of Commerce Internet Policy
Taskforce released a series of recommendations incorporating stakeholder input for
ways the government could incentivize use of the framework. The U.S. Chamber of
Commerce has also suggested a number of incentives. What incentives do you think
would have the biggest impact on business behavior?

Answer. The U.S. Chamber generally separates the cybersecurity incentives discussion into two categories—(1) incentives related to information sharing and (2) incentives related to using risk management tools like the National Institute of Standards and Technology (NIST) *Framework for Improving Critical Infrastructure Cybersecurity* (the framework).

First, incentives spurring bidirectional information about cyber threats among
multiple government and private entities are most important to Chamber members.
The Chamber needs Congress to send a bill to the president that gives businesses
legal certainty that they are protected from liability when voluntarily sharing and
receiving threat indicators and countermeasures in real time and taking actions to
mitigate cyberattacks.

The legislation also needs to offer protections related to public disclosure, regulatory, and antitrust matters in order to increase the timely exchange of information
among public and private entities. The Chamber believes that legislation needs to
safeguard privacy and civil liberties and establish appropriate roles for civilian and
intelligence agencies. At the time of this writing, the draft Cybersecurity Information Sharing Act of 2015 (CISA) goes the furthest compared with other proposals
in addressing the legal and policy priorities that the Chamber has been pushing for
several years.

Second, the Chamber appreciates that the administration is considering a limited
number of incentives for the private sector to voluntarily use the framework.[1] However, the most important incentive that the administration and lawmakers could extend to companies is the assurance that the cybersecurity framework would remain
collaborative, flexible, and innovative over the long term. The Chamber believes that
the presence of these qualities, or the lack thereof, would be a key determinant to
participation by businesses, including critical infrastructure, in using the framework.

Ultimately, policymakers need to meet with each critical infrastructure sector to
discuss what businesses need to potentially encourage greater use of the cybersecurity framework. The right incentives may be available or they may need to be created. In April 2013, the Chamber sent NIST a letter regarding businesses' use of
the framework and the role of incentives.

Here are some incentives that are frequently discussed by public and private sector stakeholders, which the Chamber is willing to consider:

- *Extending liability protections (information sharing).* Businesses seek to participate in the online equivalent of a Neighborhood Watch program for cybersecurity. Companies' security professionals want to exchange cyber threat information
  and vulnerabilities with their peers and government—but they fear being sanc-
  tioned for doing the right thing. The Chamber strongly urges Congress to pass
  an information-sharing bill this year with strong protections related to liability,
  public disclosure, regulatory, and antitrust concerns.

- *Extending liability protections (framework).* Congress may consider extending liability protections to companies that voluntarily adopt the cybersecurity framework. This is a welcome option. However, our experience with S. 3414, the Cybersecurity Act of 2012, demonstrates that the level of protection authorized in
  the bill (*i.e.,* against punitive damages sought in a lawsuit) was relatively weak.
  The bill provided insufficient protection to sway businesses' decision making in
  favor of the legislation. In other words, the stick was considerably bigger than
  the carrot.

- *Extending liability protections (SAFETY Act).* The administration and Congress
  are expected to assess how the Support Anti-terrorism by Fostering Effective
  Technologies Act of 2002 (SAFETY Act) could allow for legal liability protections
  for providers of qualified cybersecurity technologies. The act is intended to expand the development and commercialization of innovative products and services to mitigate significant cybersecurity incidents. This may require a review
  and possibly a modification of the events that would trigger SAFETY Act coverage and the types of technologies and services that would be covered. House

---

[1] *www.whitehouse.gov/blog/2015/02/02/strengthening-cyber-risk-management*

cybersecurity legislation in the 113th Congress (H.R. 3696) contained such as provision.

- *Harmonizing cybersecurity regulations.* Information-security requirements should not be cumulative. The Chamber believes it is valuable that agencies and departments are urged under the 2013 cybersecurity executive order (EO) to report to the Office of Management and Budget any critical infrastructure subject to "ineffective, conflicting, or excessively burdensome cybersecurity requirements." The Chamber urges the administration and Congress to prioritize eliminating burdensome regulations on businesses. One solution could entail giving businesses credit for information security regimes that exist in their respective sectors. It is positive that Michael Daniel, the administration's lead cyber official, has made harmonizing existing cyber regulations with the framework a priority in a February 2, 2015, blog.

- *Leveraging Federal procurement.* The Chamber generally supports a government procurement process that rewards vendors that follow industry-recognized cybersecurity guidance. However, we are concerned about the unintended consequences of procurement incentives, such as a program that leads to one-size-fits-all outcomes or to artificially chosen technology winners and losers. The Chamber urges the administration to be mindful of how procurement incentives, however beneficial in the American context, could prompt foreign governments to emulate this policy as a way of restricting U.S. companies' access to overseas markets.

  The Chamber cautions against expanding the scope of section 8 of the 2013 cybersecurity EO.[2] The administration recognizes that it should not determine how companies design, develop, and manufacture their technology and products. There are well-established laws and policies on the books to ensure that government procurement processes leverage—rather than duplicate and weaken—industry-led, international technology standards and best practices.

- *Making the research and development (R&D) tax credit permanent.* Congress should make the R&D tax credit permanent to help businesses adopt a multi-layered cybersecurity program that matures over time in relation to risks. This is particularly important for small and midsize company owners and operators who typically lack the money and human talent to deploy a sophisticated program.

Question 2. The U.S. Chamber has noted that standards are most effective when developed and recognized globally, which can help prevent the burden of multiple, conflicting jurisdictional requirements.

The Cybersecurity Enhancement Act (Public Law 113–274) recognized NIST's convening role in international standards development and required NIST to consult with foreign governments and international organizations to support the framework development process. How can the U.S. Chamber leverage its members' global operations to facilitate this international alignment?

Answer. The Chamber is urging U.S. and foreign government officials to align international cybersecurity regimes with the framework. Many Chamber members operate globally. We applaud NIST for actively meeting with foreign officials urging them to embrace the framework. Like NIST, the Chamber believes that efforts to improve the cybersecurity of the public and private sectors should reflect the borderless and interconnected nature of our digital environment.

Standards, guidance, and best practices relevant to cybersecurity are typically industry driven and adopted on a voluntary basis. They are most effective when developed and recognized globally. Such an approach would avoid burdening multinational enterprises with the requirements of multiple, and often conflicting, jurisdictions.

The Chamber is planning to hold meetings in May in Berlin and Brussels with U.S. and European public officials and industry representatives to discuss issues of mutual interest including the cybersecurity framework, digital innovation, international data flows, and data privacy. Our organization intends to engage additional countries and regions globally.

Meanwhile, the Chamber urges the administration to organize opportunities for stakeholders to participate in multinational discussions. We encourage the Federal Government to work with international partners and believe that these discussions should be stakeholder driven and occur on a routine basis.

---

[2] *www.whitehouse.gov/the-press-office/2013/02/12/executive-order-improving-critical-infra-structure-cybersecurity*

RESPONSE TO WRITTEN QUESTIONS SUBMITTED BY HON. ROY BLUNT TO
ANN M. BEAUCHESNE

Question 1. You state in your testimony that the NIST framework is incomplete
without Congress enacting information-sharing legislation. Can you elaborate on
this? Is it fair to say that, in the same sense the NIST framework is voluntary, that
the sharing of cyber threat indicators must be voluntary as well?

Answer. I would like to begin with part two of this question by saying that cybersecurity information sharing must be voluntary. The U.S. Chamber would oppose
any program mandating that companies report cyber threat data to the government,
save for what companies agree to via contract.

Improving information sharing should be job No. 1 for policymakers. The National
Institute of Standards and Technology's (NIST's) *Framework for Improving Critical
Infrastructure Cybersecurity* (the framework) would be incomplete without enacting
information-sharing legislation that removes legal and regulatory barriers to rapidly
exchanging data about threats to U.S. companies. On January 27, 35 associations,
including the Chamber, urged the Senate to quickly pass a cybersecurity information-sharing bill. The Senate Intelligence committee passed in July the Cybersecurity Information Sharing Act (CISA) of 2014, a smart and workable bill, which earned
broad bipartisan support.

Recent cyber incidents underscore the need for legislation to help businesses improve their awareness of cyber threats and enhance their protection and response
capabilities. The Chamber urges Congress to send a bill to the president that gives
businesses legal certainty that they have safe harbor against frivolous lawsuits
when voluntarily sharing and receiving threat indicators and countermeasures in
real time with multiple private and public entities, as well as when monitoring information systems to mitigate cyberattacks. The legislation also needs to offer protections related to public disclosure, regulatory, and antitrust matters in order to
increase the timely exchange of technical cyber threat indicators (CTIs) and countermeasures among public and private entities.

The Chamber further believes that legislation needs to safeguard privacy and civil
liberties and establish appropriate roles for civilian and intelligence agencies. For
example, businesses must remove personal information from CTIs before sharing indicators. Private entities must share "electronic mail or media, an interactive form
on an Internet website, or a real time, automated process between information systems" with DHS—a civilian entity—if they are to be offered protection from liability.

CISA, which is sponsored by Sens. Richard Burr and Dianne Feinstein, reflects
practical compromises among many stakeholders on these issues. At the time of this
writing, the measure was marked up on March 12 and reported to the full Senate
on a strong bipartisan vote of 14–1. The Chamber urges the Senate to pass CISA
soon.

Question 2. In your testimony, you cited the need for the U.S. government to raise
the costs on malicious cyber-attackers through an intelligent and forceful deterrence
strategy. Can you elaborate what a cyber-deterrence strategy should look like?

Answer. The Chamber is reviewing actions that businesses and government can
take to deter nefarious actors that threaten to empty bank accounts, steal trade secrets, or damage vital infrastructures. While our organization has not formally endorsed the report, the U.S. Department of State's International Security Advisory
Board (ISAB) issued in July draft recommendations regarding cooperation and deterrence in cyberspace.

The ISAB's recommendations—including cooperating on crime as a first step, exploring global consensus on the rules of the road, enhancing governments' situational awareness through information sharing, combating IP theft, expanding education and capacity building, promoting attribution and prosecution, and leading by
example—are sensible and worthy of further review by cybersecurity stakeholders.[1]

The Chamber believes that the United States needs to coherently shift the costs
associated with cyberattacks in ways that are legal, swift, and proportionate relative
to the risks and threats. Policymakers need to help the law enforcement community,
which is a key asset to the business community but numerically overmatched compared with illicit hackers.[2]

The Chamber would welcome working with you, other lawmakers, and the administration on establishing an effective cyber deterrence strategy, using an array of
policy tools that the United States lacks.

---

[1] The ISAB report is available at *www.state.gov/documents/organization/229235.pdf.*
[2] The Chamber argued for a clear cyber deterrence strategy in its December 2013 letter to
NIST on the framework. See *http://csrc.nist.gov/cyberframework/framework\comments/2013
1213\ann_beauchesne\uschamber.pdf.*

Question 3. The framework itself is voluntary and based upon a risk management model, as opposed to compliance with rote standards. Wouldn't the concept of a mandatory survey be counter to the voluntary approach adopted by NIST, and could it impact the use of the framework if private sector owners and operators of critical infrastructure view using the framework as being linked to new reporting requirements? Please provide your perspective on the mandatory survey proposal.

Answer. The framework is a remarkable public-private achievement. NIST worked closely with the Chamber's Cybersecurity Working Group and other private sector organizations to develop the framework. NIST treated the business community as a genuine partner as it tackled a tough assignment in ways that should serve as a model for other agencies and departments.

Generally, the Chamber does not survey its members, which we have also communicated to Sen. Nelson. However, the Chamber is committing substantial resources to promoting the framework to its membership and the wider business community. As highlighted in my testimony, the Chamber has organized an extensive, ongoing cybersecurity education and advocacy campaign—*Improving Today, Protecting Tomorrow* ™—partnering with state and local chambers to host events in Chicago, Austin, Seattle, and Phoenix.

The Chamber also hosted a number of events in Washington, D.C., including America's Small Business Summit 2014 and the Third Annual Cybersecurity Summit, where discussion of the framework was prominently featured. Further, we are planning events this year to build on the success of the 2014 campaign.

Use of the framework is voluntary—not mandatory—which is why many businesses and public-sector organizations, such as county IT departments, have embraced it. Industry's interest in cybersecurity and the framework is robust and expanding. Michael Daniel, White House special assistant to the president and cybersecurity coordinator, said in September 2014 at the Chamber's third cyber roundtable in Seattle that industry's response to the framework has been "phenomenal."

The Chamber supported the Cybersecurity Enhancement Act of 2014 (S. 1353, P.L. 113–274), sponsored by Sens. Rockefeller and Thune and signed into law on December 18, 2014. The act directs the comptroller general to conduct a study assessing the extent to which "sectors of critical infrastructure have adopted a voluntary, industry-led set of standards," and "the reasons behind the decisions" of critical infrastructure to do so. The Chamber believes that this study would offer much more insight about framework use than a mandatory survey of individual firms.

It is worth adding that critical infrastructure sectors are keenly aware of and supportive of the framework and similar risk management tools. The Chamber understands that critical infrastructures at "greatest risk" (CIGR) have been identified and engaged by administration officials under the terms of the 2013 cybersecurity executive order (EO).[3] If the United States is to build a more secure cyber future, the Chamber urges you and other government officials to ensure that all resources, particularly the latest cyber threat information, are available to CIGR to counter increasing and advanced threats.

At the time of this writing, it is not clear that Federal entities such as the Department of Homeland Security (DHS) have utilized all resources at their disposal to help CIGR mitigate expensive cyberattacks emanating from highly advanced and nefarious actors. Policymakers have not sufficiently acknowledged this expensive, practical reality. Nation-states or their proxies and other sophisticated criminal actors are apparently hacking businesses with impunity. This needs to stop.

Question 4. Ms. Beauchesne, in your testimony you cite the need to harmonize preexisting regulations on cybersecurity. Please submit for record specific details regarding which agencies and what regulations are duplicative, burdensome, inconsistent, or otherwise in conflict with the NIST framework and our goal of better cybersecurity.

Answer. Information-security requirements should not be cumulative. The Chamber believes it is valuable that agencies and departments are urged under the 2013 cybersecurity EO to report to the Office of Management and Budget any critical infrastructure subject to "ineffective, conflicting, or excessively burdensome cybersecurity requirements." We urge the administration and Congress to prioritize eliminating burdensome regulations on businesses.[4] Thus, it is positive that Michael

---

[3] *www.whitehouse.gov/the-press-office/2013/02/12/executive-order-improving-critical-infrastructure-cybersecurity*

[4] The business community already complies with multiple information security rules. Among the regulatory requirements impacting businesses of all sizes are the Chemical Facilities Anti-Terrorism Standards (CFATS), the Federal Energy Regulatory Commission-North American Reliability Corporation Critical Information Protection (FERC–NERC CIP) standards, the Gramm-Leach-Bliley Act (GLBA), the Health Insurance Portability and Accountability Act (HIPAA), and

Daniel, the administration's lead cyber official, has made harmonizing preexisting cyber regulations with the framework a priority.[5]

The Chamber would defer to leading sector associations and companies to determine what works best for them vis-à-vis government regulators. The examples that follow partially illustrate the challenges involved in streamlining regulations.

First, some businesses in the communications sector—made up of broadcasting, cable, wireline, wireless, and satellite segments—believe that agency duplication is a growing concern. Multiple agencies—including DHS, the Federal Communications Commission (FCC), and the National Telecommunications and Information Administration (NTIA)[6]—address cybersecurity in the communications sector. Whether it is the communications sector or another one, quality cybersecurity expertise is hard to attract and retain. Cyber personnel and their business colleagues (*e.g.,* with legal and risk management duties) should not be unduly stressed battling both advanced hackers and Federal regulators. Regulatory overlap could easily lead to conflicting rules and the splintering of industry resources, which would be detrimental to cybersecurity. Such a problem is not unique to the communications sector.

Second, financial institutions offer numerous products and services that subject them to multiple cybersecurity and information privacy programs, including the Gramm-Leach-Bliley Act (GLBA) and various rules and guidance issued by Federal and state regulators. Federal financial sector regulators work toward harmonizing their mandates across agencies through bodies like the Federal Financial Institutions Examination Council (FFIEC)[7] and the Financial and Banking Information Infrastructure Committee (FBIIC). Nevertheless, agencies commonly leave the interpretation of rules and guidance documents to individual agency officials who may interpret them differently, often leading to confusing or conflicting recommendations.

Further, beyond the Federal level, there are several state-based financial regulatory entities that create their own guidance and have oversight responsibilities, adding to the regulatory mix. The financial services industry needs improved consistency and clarity among their various regulators to minimize costs while maximizing business safety and soundness.

Third, the natural gas sector is impacted by a long list of recommended practices, standards, and guidelines—including the DHS Transportation Security Administration (TSA) *Pipeline Security Guidelines* (2011),[8] the Department of Energy's (DOE's) Cybersecurity Capability Maturity Model (C2M2),[9] and DHS' Cyber Security Evaluation Tool (CSET®)—which are employed by industry operators to bolster their cybersecurity posture and resilience in an all-hazards context. Natural gas companies have worked diligently to use one or more of these standards and recommended practices. However, as companies are increasingly pressured by government agencies to use multiple tools, cybersecurity can become more of a record-keeping and compliance exercise rather than an exercise in advancing legitimate security.

The Chamber hopes that the new Cybersecurity Forum for Independent and Executive Branch Regulators can help, according to its fall 2014 charter, "identify and explore opportunities to align, leverage, and deconflict cross-sector regulatory authorities' approaches and promote cybersecurity protection."[10] We would like to maintain a dialogue with your office and the Commerce committee as the administration and the interagency forum tackle the regulatory streamlining initiative tied to the framework.

———

RESPONSE TO WRITTEN QUESTIONS SUBMITTED BY HON. BILL NELSON TO
ANN M. BEAUCHESNE

Question 1. I want to follow up on the request I made to you at the hearing. Of the 200 or so members that make up the National Security Task Force, how many

the Sarbanes-Oxley (SO$_X$) Act. The Securities and Exchange Commission (SEC) issued guidance in October 2011 outlining how and when companies should report hacking incidents and cybersecurity risks. Corporations also comply with many non-U.S. requirements, which add to the regulatory mix.

[5] *www.whitehouse.gov/blog/2015/02/02/strengthening-cyber-risk-management*
[6] *www.ntia.doc.gov/press-release/2015/iptf-seeks-comment-key-cybersecurity-issues*
[7] *http://ithandbook.ffiec.gov/it-booklets/business-continuity-planning.aspx*
[8] *www.tsa.gov/assets/pdf/guidelines\final\apr2011.pdf*
[9] *http://energy.gov/oe/services/cybersecurity/cybersecurity-capability-maturity-model-c2m2-program/cybersecurity*
[10] *http://pbadupws.nrc.gov/docs/ML1428/ML14288A568.pdf; http://pbadupws.nrc.gov/docs/ML1501/ML15014A296.pdf*

of them have implemented the framework? How many members in your general membership have implemented the framework?

Answer. The U.S. Chamber of Commerce believes that the *Framework for Improving Critical Infrastructure Cybersecurity* (the framework) is a remarkable public-private achievement. The National Institute of Standards and Technology (NIST) worked closely with the Chamber's Cybersecurity Working Group and other private sector organizations to develop the framework. NIST treated the business community as a genuine partner as it tackled a tough assignment in ways that should serve as a model for other agencies and departments.

Generally, the Chamber does not survey its members. Yet, the Chamber is committing substantial resources to promoting the framework to its membership and the wider business community. As highlighted in my testimony, the Chamber has organized an extensive, ongoing cybersecurity education and advocacy campaign—*Improving Today, Protecting Tomorrow* ™—partnering with state and local chambers to host events in Chicago, Austin, Seattle, and Phoenix.

The Chamber also hosted a number of events in Washington, D.C., including America's Small Business Summit 2014 and the Third Annual Cybersecurity Summit, where discussion of the framework was prominently featured. Further, we are planning events this year to build on the success of the 2014 campaign.

Use of the framework is voluntary, not mandatory, which is why many businesses and public-sector organizations, such as county IT departments, have embraced it. Industry's interest in cybersecurity and the framework is robust and expanding. Michael Daniel, White House special assistant to the president and cybersecurity coordinator, said in September 2014 at the Chamber's third cyber roundtable in Seattle that industry's response to the framework has been "phenomenal."

The Chamber supported the Cybersecurity Enhancement Act of 2014 (S. 1353, P.L. 113–274), sponsored by Sens. Rockefeller and Thune and signed into law on December 18, 2014. The act directs the comptroller general to conduct a study assessing the extent to which "sectors of critical infrastructure have adopted a voluntary, industry-led set of standards," and "the reasons behind the decisions" of critical infrastructure to do so. The Chamber believes that this study would offer much more insight about framework use.

It is worth adding that critical infrastructure sectors are keenly aware of and supportive of the framework and similar risk management tools. The Chamber understands that critical infrastructures at "greatest risk" (CIGR) have been identified and engaged by administration officials under the terms of the 2013 cybersecurity executive order (EO).[1] If the United States is to build a more secure cyber future, the Chamber urges you and other government officials to ensure that all resources, particularly the latest cyber threat information, are available to CIGR to counter increasing and advanced threats.

At the time of this writing, it is not clear that Federal entities such as the Department of Homeland Security (DHS) have utilized all resources at their disposal to help CIGR mitigate expensive cyberattacks emanating from highly advanced and nefarious actors. Policymakers have not sufficiently acknowledged this expensive, practical reality. Nation-states or their proxies and other sophisticated criminal actors are apparently hacking businesses with impunity. This needs to stop.

In addition to having policymakers acknowledge cost concerns, the Chamber would welcome working with you, other lawmakers, and the administration on establishing an intelligent and forceful deterrence strategy, using an array of policy tools that the United States lacks.

Question 2. What is the prevalence of cyber insurance policies among members of the U.S. Chamber of Commerce? And what is the amount of annual payouts under those policies?

Answer. The prevalence of cyber insurance among Chamber members is unknown. Typically, the Chamber does not ask its members about such matters because this information is relatively sensitive.

We note, however, that more than 50 major insurance providers now offer cyber insurance coverage. According to a Marsh Risk Management Research report, demand for cyber insurance grew by 21 percent across all industries in 2013, compared with 2012, and the pace is increasing. Financial institutions accounted for the largest percentage—nearly 30 percent—of that increase. Other data-intensive sectors, including retail/wholesale and professional services, saw increases of 19 percent and 13 percent, respectively. It appears that demand for cyber insurance is

---

[1] *www.whitehouse.gov/the-press-office/2013/02/12/executive-order-improving-critical-infrastructure-cybersecurity*

booming as a result of a number of high-profile hacks and data breaches, spurring explosive growth in what is approximately a $2 billion industry.

The Chamber applauds the insurance industry for developing market-driven policies to help businesses mitigate losses from a variety of cyber incidents, including data breaches, business interruption, and network damage. Business purchases of cybersecurity insurance should go hand in hand with investments in cybersecurity.

Cyber insurance risk is challenging to measure, model, and price. Nevertheless, growing awareness of the cybersecurity framework and almost daily headlines about cyber incidents have stimulated industry's interest in cyber insurance. A healthy cyber insurance market should play a role in businesses' reducing the number of successful cyberattacks by implementing risk management tools in return for more coverage.

The Chamber supports a growing cyber insurance market, which is nascent compared with more established lines such as auto, life, and health. But, the Chamber would not support public policies either compelling insurers to offer cyber insurance or mandating that firms buy cyber insurance.

The Chamber plans to promote cyber risk management tools, including cyber insurance, as part of its national roundtable cybersecurity series. The campaign emphasizes growing awareness of the framework—particularly recommending that businesses of all sizes and sectors adopt fundamental Internet security practices—and teaming up with law enforcement and entities like DHS.

If the campaign comes to a Florida city, the Chamber would welcome having you as a keynote speaker.

————

RESPONSE TO WRITTEN QUESTIONS SUBMITTED BY HON. JOHN THUNE TO PAUL N. SMOCER

Question 1. The financial services sector is a leader in cyber threat information-sharing innovation, as evidenced by the successful collaboration via the FS–ISAC and the creation of Soltra Edge, a new threat intelligence-sharing software platform. What are the key principles that cyber threat information sharing legislation must include to eliminate existing constraints on the activities of the FS–ISAC and Soltra Edge?

Answer. The financial services sector realizes that in order to appropriately defend itself, threat information sharing is key.

The FS–ISAC coordinates information sharing today among its member institutions, with industry associations, and between financial institutions and the Federal Government, law enforcement and other critical infrastructure sectors. Information is shared through the traffic light protocol (TLP), which allows recipients of the threat data to know the sensitivity of the information they receive and their ability to share. This allows data to be distributed to the right audiences in a more secure and trusted format. Soltra Edge expands on the FS–ISAC's trust model for cyber threat information sharing in that Soltra Edge is an automation platform that collects, distills, and transfers threat intelligence from and to a variety of other sources, including, but not limited to the FS–ISAC.

Because of the level of current sharing that occurs, the financial services sector is often and rightly credited as being one of leaders in cybersecurity and, particularly, cyber threat information sharing. Even at that level though, not everyone participates in sharing and even those that do at times become reticent to share. In the latter case, this is particularly true when there is some success to an attack versus just an attempt to attack. In these cases, issues of liability often influence the decisions to share freely.

One must also recognize that our sector exists in an interconnected world. As a sector, we are not an island unto ourselves. We need and rely on the sectors that provide us with power, water, telecommunications, computing, etc. A key reason for the immaturity in those sectors is concern over the potential liabilities associated with sharing such information.

To encourage better information sharing within our sector, in other sectors, between the sectors, and to the government, sensible ''Good Samaritan'' protections are needed. Without such legislation, cyber threat information sharing will not expand beyond those companies that already do so to those companies that should do so, but fear litigation and potential reputational damage for sharing. In particular, we believe that in order to protect current initiatives, such as the FS–ISAC and Soltra Edge, and to expand cyber threat sharing beyond those that already do so, legislation is needed that includes the following provisions:

• Facilitates real-time sharing to enable institutions and government to act quickly;

- Provides a targeted level of liability and disclosure protections for cyber threat information sharing and receiving between individual institutions, through existing sharing mechanisms such as our FS–ISAC, private to government, and government to private;
- Offers a good faith defense for the sharing of threat information and data;
- Provides protection from disclosure through the Freedom of Information Act or to prudential regulators;
- Facilitates the appropriate declassification of information by the intelligence agencies and expedites the issuance of clearances to appropriate private sector individuals; and
- Includes appropriate levels of privacy and civil liberties requirements.

The threat of cyber-attacks is a real and constant danger to our industry and to other critical infrastructure sectors upon which we, and the Nation as a whole, rely. The financial services industry is dedicated to improving our capacity to protect customers and their sensitive information. Effective cyber threat information sharing mitigates cyber risks to our customers, clients, partners and networks from malicious cyber activity.

Question 2. Mr. Smocer, you mentioned in your testimony that the Cybersecurity Forum for Independent and Executive Branch Regulators is looking at ways to align and harmonize with the Framework and thus streamline regulatory agencies' cybersecurity efforts regarding critical infrastructure. Can you tell me how the financial services sector will benefit from harmonizing regulatory authorities and requirements and how this Forum is facilitating such benefits?

Answer. According to the Charter for the Independent and Executive Branch Regulators, "[t]he purpose of the voluntary Cybersecurity Forum for Independent and Executive Branch Regulators (The Forum) is to increase the overall effectiveness and consistency of regulatory authorities' cybersecurity efforts pertaining to U.S. Critical Infrastructure, much of which is operated by industry and overseen by a number of Federal regulatory authorities. The Forum will enhance communication among regulatory agencies and regulated entities through the sharing of best practices and exploring ways to align, leverage, and deconflict approaches to enhance cybersecurity protections, and will establish processes to encourage coordination and consistency where multiple Agencies have regulatory authority over a common industry." We laud such an approach and hope that it bears fruit. However, as described in our response to Sen. Blunt's question, there is some cause for concern.

Simply, financial institutions are subject to various cyber security and information privacy requirements under the Gramm Leach Bliley Act and to regulatory standards and guidance issued by numerous financial regulators. In today's world, financial institutions often are multi-faceted, offering products and services that subject them to the regulatory authority of multiple agencies.

To their credit, the Federal financial sector regulators do attempt to bring some consistency to their guidance and regulatory expectations across agencies through organizations such as the Federal Financial Institutions Examination Council (FFIEC) and the Financial and Banking Information Infrastructure Committee (FBIIC). To a limited extent, this helps avoid a single organization facing multiple expectations about the same operations. Even then, agencies often leave the interpretation of that guidance to agency-specific reviewers who may interpret it differently. Moreover, beyond the Federal level, there are a plethora of state level financial regulators who create their own guidance and by law have oversight responsibilities. For financial institutions, consistency among their various regulators helps keep down costs and overhead while still assuring safety and soundness.

Beyond our industry though, the financial services sector would benefit from harmonizing regulatory standards across critical infrastructure sectors, such as telecommunications and electrical power. This would help all the sectors that rely upon each other to be able to better assess the level of cyber risk between sectors. It would better allow agencies responsible for assuring the Nation's cyber protection of the consistency of cybersecurity efforts across sectors. Practically, as the number of regulators with disparate requirements increases, the ability to train and place cybersecurity experts—already an expertise with a recognized shortage—also becomes more taxed.

RESPONSE TO WRITTEN QUESTION SUBMITTED BY HON. ROY BLUNT TO
PAUL N. SMOCER

Question. Mr. Smocer, in your testimony you mention your concerns that some
Federal and state agencies have their own approaches to regulation that do not
align with the Framework.

Please submit for record specific details regarding which agencies and what regulations are duplicative, burdensome, inconsistent, or otherwise in conflict with the
NIST framework and our goal of better cybersecurity.

Answer. As mentioned in my prior testimony, FSR/BITS is a trade association
representing the country's leading financial service companies. Under current regulatory regimes, some of our individual member institutions face regulation from the
following regulatory bodies:

• The Securities and Exchange Commission (SEC);
• FINRA;
• The Federal Reserve System;
• The Office of the Comptroller of the Currency (OCC) ;
• The Federal Deposit Insurance Corporation (FDIC);
• The Consumer Financial Protection Bureau (CFPB);
• The U.S. Commodity Futures Trading Commission (CFTC);
• State banking agencies, and
• State insurance agencies.

None of the above regulators, however, are Executive Branch agencies. Thus,
these agencies are not subject to the President's Executive Orders and they do not
have to adhere to the Administration's directives to harmonize cybersecurity regulations. Perhaps because of this, we have seen examples of agencies each asking their
own set of cybersecurity examination questions that may loosely "track" to the NIST
Cybersecurity Framework, but in substance deviate from agency to agency.

For example:

• In April 2014, the SEC's Office of Compliance Inspections and Examinations
  (OCIE) issued a risk alert in which it announced that it would be conducting
  cybersecurity-focused examinations of approximately 50+ registered broker-deal-
  ers and investment advisors. In this same risk alert (*http://www.sec.gov/ocie/
  announcement/Cybersecurity+Risk+Alert++%2526+Appendix+-+4.15.14.pdf*),
  OCIE stated that "some" of its questions would "track information outlined in
  the 'Framework for Improving Critical Infrastructure Cybersecurity." Of the 28
  example questions with subparts not all did.

• On November 3, 2014, the FFIEC issued its "FFIEC Cybersecurity Assessment
  General Observations." This document detailed the FFIEC's cybersecurity ex-
  aminations of 500+ community institutions and provided cybersecurity areas to
  focus on and certain questions to consider when considering cybersecurity risk.
  It did not, however, tie these focus area or questions to the NIST Cybersecurity
  Framework.[1]

• Without a reference to the NIST Cybersecurity Framework, the New York State
  Department of Financial Services issued an "examination guidance" to all New
  York State chartered or licensed banking institutions on December 10, 2014,
  stating that it would be conducting "new targeted cybersecurity preparedness
  assessments" of these entities.[2] In this announcement, the Department also announced that as part of that assessment it would be asking 12 specific questions.[3]

• On February 3, 2015, FINRA issued its "Report on Cybersecurity Practices."[4]
  Like the SEC, it referenced the NIST Cybersecurity Framework. However, in
  detailing cybersecurity best practices that firms should implement, it did not
  "map" such practices back to the NIST Cybersecurity Framework categories or
  subcategories. Such an exercise would be left to an individual firm that wished
  to compare the Framework against this new set of cybersecurity best practices.

We certainly are glad to see an increasing focus on cybersecurity by agencies that
play an important role in protecting the financial services industry. However, lack

---

[1]   *https://www.ffiec.gov/press/PDF/FFIEC\Cybersecurity\Assessment\Observations.pdf*
[2] *http://www.dfs.ny.gov/about/press2014/pr1412101.htm*
[3]   *http://www.dfs.ny.gov/banking/bil-2014-10-10\cyber\security.pdf*
[4]   *http://www.finra.org/web/groups/industry/@ip/@reg/@guide/documents/industry/
p602363.pdf*

of harmonization between agencies and with the Cybersecurity Framework means that regulated organizations must continually reinvest their resources not in defending themselves against cyber assaults, but in assessing and reassessing themselves against multiple agency expectations. That is simply not an effective approach.

———

RESPONSE TO WRITTEN QUESTIONS SUBMITTED BY HON. BILL NELSON TO PAUL N. SMOCER

Question 1. Some members of the Financial Services Roundtable sell insurance products that cover financial losses associated with cyberattacks. Do you have any data on how much is being paid out to insureds as a result of losses from cyberattacks?

Answer. FSR does not have, nor do we collect, data on what our member companies pay out under various cyber insurance policies.

Question 2. Last week, the press reported on a massive hacking ring that is alleged to have stolen up to $1 billion from banks in numerous countries, including the United States. The news, which emerged from a report written by Kaspersky Lab, is just the latest in a string of massive hacks and breaches in recent years, including last year's breach at JPMorgan Chase. At what point does consumer dissatisfaction with cyberattacks affect a company's decisions to devote more resources to cybersecurity?

Answer. Specific to the report from Kaspersky Lab, FSR has been aware of the analysis that has underlied this report since early January. Our BITS division has distributed such information to security experts within our member companies. In addition, the FS–ISAC has distributed information to the entire financial sector. At this point in time, we are unaware of incidences where this malware has harmed our member companies or their customers. Like all cyber-attacks, FSR will continue to monitor these threats and work with our member companies and the FS–ISAC to share threat information and assist our members in responding to them and in protecting customers.

More broadly, the Kaspersky report and other recent security trends point to the fact that the threats are rapidly growing. However, it is important to recognize that financial institutions' investment in cyber is a long-established practice. While recent events help feed the continual reassessment of cyber risk within institutions that, in turn, help drive investments in cyber protections, it would be improper to suggest that recent events have somehow been a stimulus that awoke the sector to this risk. The sector has focused on this risk for decades.

As I noted in my testimony, the current cyber threat environment is grim. Each day, cyber risk grows as attacks increase in number, pace, and complexity. We are no longer in the days wherein the threat was confined to individual hacktivists and fraudsters. We are now in an era of attacks by not only organized crime syndicates, but also nation-states. Correspondingly, the attacks have grown beyond webpage vandalism and fraud into large-scale attacks that threaten the availability of services to citizens and threaten the privacy and accuracy of their information. Our sector is increasingly concerned with these threats, particularly with the potential for attacks that could undermine the integrity of the financial system through data manipulation or destruction. This growing threat affects all institutions in our sector regardless of size or type of financial institution including large and small, banks, credit unions, insurers and investment firms. Increasingly, and as we have recently witnessed, other sectors face these same threats.

Being a focus of attacks is certainly one reason why the financial sector has historically led the way in making huge investments in not only security infrastructure and the best-qualified people to maintain the systems, but also in driving collaboration across industries and with the government. The primary reason for these investments though is the recognition that our customers trust us to protect them— to protect their investments, their records and their information. Individual financial institutions invest in personnel, infrastructure, services, and top of the line security protocols to protect their customers and themselves and to respond to cyber-attacks. These investments protect the individual institutions and their customers. The level and nature of cybersecurity investments are subjects of discussions within both the C-suite of institutions and with their boards. Institution executives know they are responsible for managing risk in their companies, and recognize that cyber-risk in particular bears special attention. Directors understand their oversight role in assuring management is fulfilling those responsibilities. Both management's and directors' ability to assess and respond to cyber risk is also the subject of review by financial regulators.

Question 3. What is the prevalence of cyber insurance policies among members of the Financial Services Roundtable? And what is the amount of annual payouts under those policies?

Answer. While we do not have data specific to our members, our research has revealed that 2014 marked an important milestone in the growth of cyber insurance, with a significant jump in both the number of companies offering cyber insurance and the number of firms buying cyber insurance. Currently, over fifty major insurance providers now offer cyber liability insurance coverage. Demand for that insurance rose by 21 percent across all industries in 2013 compared to 2012, with financial institutions representing the biggest increase of 29 percent in coverage buying. In 2014 that pace doubled, in some areas tripled, in what suddenly has become a $2 billion industry.

Several developments contribute to the growth in cyber insurance.

1. The recent increase in cyber incidents, both in number and severity, including a string of high-profile hacks and data breaches.

2. A growing realization that although steps can be taken to minimize the likelihood of experiencing a successful cyber-attack and the severity of the loss if the attack succeeds, its occurrence cannot be entirely eliminated, especially if the enterprise becomes the target of a sophisticated, persistent adversary. It is becoming accepted that cybersecurity is similar to healthcare in the sense that one can take precautions, but not prevent entirely.

3. Increased appreciation and understanding of best practices, such as those found in the NIST Cybersecurity Framework, has improved underwriting ability, which has bolstered supply.

Regarding payouts by member company insurers, as noted in my response to question #1 above, we do not have, nor do we collect, data on FSR member company payouts on cyber insurance policies.

———

RESPONSE TO WRITTEN QUESTIONS SUBMITTED BY HON. JOHN THUNE TO JEFFERSON H. ENGLAND

Question 1. In August of 2013, the Department of Commerce Internet Policy Taskforce released a series of recommendations incorporating stakeholder input for ways the government could incentivize use of the Framework. Some of the potential incentives mentioned include engaging cyber insurance companies, studying tort liability, identifying opportunities for regulatory streamlining, further research and development initiatives, government procurement, and technical assistance. What incentives do you think would have the biggest impact on business behavior?

Answer. As a small business, we recognize that the greatest incentive is the ability to attract and retain customers by demonstrating capability in our cybersecurity practices and the ability to enter into contracts with our vendors to deliver secure services to our customers. The market already provides strong cybersecurity incentives.

However, tort liability review would have a powerful impact on business behavior. Individuals who attack our networks are criminals. State sponsored attacks on our networks are acts of war. As businesses, we need to know that if we employ reasonable cybersecurity practices that our government has our back when it comes to brining the perpetrators to justice. Not only will evildoers be more discouraged from committing cybercrime, but business and consumers will by extension have greater protection. Businesses know that they need to accept responsibility. and providing protections from liability.

There are already many creative ideas designed to protect an individual's identity. Examples include multi-factor authentification when accessing personal information, cyber "keys" that are required to unlock certain personal information, and virtual information that is a proxy for real information so that the need for safeguarding the virtual information is less relevant. Government sponsorship of research and development initiatives and government procurement are also ways that can incentivize business to reach beyond what they may already be doing. In the rural telephone industry, recovery on certain cybersecurity expenditures is not allowed via the universal service fund and yet we are required to provide defined levels of Internet service. There is a disconnect in our industry that needs to be addressed.

Cyber insurance companies already have a business imperative to "incentivize" the market because of the risk they themselves are assuming by insuring companies conducting business over the internet, so I do not believe there is a need for government to engage them in this space unless it is to be a lessons learned exercise.

It is my experience that business tends to reach out to peers and suppliers for recommendations and assistance so I cannot speak to the value of Federal technical assistance.

I would also caution against grants for cybersecurity improvements as I believe this model to be a disincentive. Grants are typically awarded on a needs basis potentially causing businesses that are currently engaged in improvement (on their own dime) to cease all improvement until they receive grant dollars. The result is a race to the bottom in terms of cyber security quality because improvements may be limited to the availability of grant dollars as distributed.

Question 2. What role, if any, do you think your industry regulator, the Federal Communications Commission, should have with respect to the Framework and cybersecurity regulations or guidelines in general?

Answer. I believe there is a significant role that the FCC can play with respect to the framework and cybersecurity regulations or guidelines in general.

First and foremost, there needs to be continued education within our industry regarding the availability of the framework and its benefits to telecommunications providers. Staff availability and encouragement is critical for more widespread adoption. Creating an atmosphere of fear and regulation is counterproductive.

Second, the FCC can and should recognize that the framework itself (let alone organizational adoption) is still in its infancy and needs the proper time to grow and evolve into a meaningful tool. I (and other employees of Silver Star Communications) participate as members of the Communications Security, Reliability and Interoperability Council (CSRIC) Working Group IV which was created with the primary purpose of developing voluntary mechanisms that provide macro-level assurance to the Federal Communications Commission (FCC) and the public that communication providers are taking the necessary corporate and operational measures to manage cybersecurity risks across the enterprise. The outcomes from this organization have been impressive, including widespread industry participation and meaningful industry suggestions and practical solutions, including a set of specific guidance to small and medium sized businesses that face very different challenges than the much larger communications companies. The FCC has played an important role in contributing to the outcomes of this working group and has been able to gain important visibility regarding industry progress from this group.

Third, the FCC can be a government advocate for communications providers with respect to tracking down and bringing criminals and state sponsored attackers to justice. The easy solution is to play the hard hand and penalize business through regulation and liability but this approach only treats the symptoms without addressing the cause of the problem.

Finally, I believe that the FCC has a responsibility to uphold the original scope of Executive Order 13636 and stand firm in the position that cybersecurity improvements should be voluntary in nature. Regulation implies that at some point (typically a reporting period) there is a static state in regards to cybersecurity, that somehow an organization is complete or done when the requirements are met. Cyber security activities are far too dynamic and businesses need to respond and even fail in their attempts to improve. The market rewards businesses who make decisions to make commerce a safer cyber experience. The FCC should recognize that things will go wrong. There will be more cybersecurity breaches. With each one, there are cries for improved regulation or to hold someone (excepting the criminals who carried out the attack) responsible without drawing attention to the fact that at the same time there are amazing advancements made in protecting information by organizations who are voluntarily adopting practices to be more competitive. I would add that because of the existing business imperative, these advancements will always outpace regulation. The consequence is that there is extreme waste of resources both on the part of businesses performing outdated activities to be compliant with regulation and by the regulating body enforcing outdated measures.

RESPONSE TO WRITTEN QUESTION SUBMITTED BY HON. ROY BLUNT TO
DR. JAMES A. LEWIS

Question. The Framework itself is voluntary and based upon a risk management model, as opposed to compliance with rote standards.

Wouldn't the concept of a mandatory survey be counter to the voluntary approach adopted by NIST, and could it impact the use of the Framework if private sector owners and operators of critical infrastructure view using the Framework as being linked to new reporting requirements?

Answer. The NIST Framework is part of a larger approach to cybersecurity created by the February 2013 Executive Order (EO) 13636 (*http://www.whitehouse.gov*

/the-press-office/2013/02/12/executive-order-improving-critical-infrastructure-cyber security). It is a standards-based approach reinforced by information sharing and partnerships between critical infrastructure companies and sector-specific agencies. The Framework must be put in the larger EO context to be understood. The EO instructed that:

- NIST develop a voluntary cybersecurity framework (Section 7);
- The Secretaries of Treasury and Commerce identify possible incentives for better cybersecurity (Section 8);
- The Departments of Homeland Security and Justice, and the Director of National Intelligence take steps to improve information sharing (the subject of a February 2105 Executive Order) (Section 4);
- That all agencies integrate strong privacy and civil liberties protections into cybersecurity initiatives to secure critical infrastructure (Section 7), and
- The White House, DHS, and agencies responsible for regulating the security of critical infrastructure review and report on the adequacy of the Framework and of existing regulation for cybersecurity (Section 10).

The EO already has a two-part reporting requirement. The first requirement was for agencies to determine whether and how existing regulation could be streamlined and aligned with the NIST Framework. Executive Branch departments and agencies with responsibility for regulating private-sector critical infrastructure were tasked to assess whether existing regulatory authority was sufficient to meet the objectives of the Framework and identify what changes, if any, were needed. At the conclusion of the review, the White House determined last May that existing regulatory requirements, combined with strong, voluntary partnerships, could mitigate risks to critical infrastructure (*http://www.whitehouse.gov/blog/2014/05/22/assessing-cybersecurity-regulations*).

The EO also calls for agencies, in consultation with critical infrastructure owners and operators, to determine by September 2016 if cybersecurity requirements are ineffective, conflicting, or excessively burdensome. This 2016 reporting will provide data to assess whether if the Framework is useful or not. The areas for further consideration include deciding if any action is needed before 2016, and ensuring that any review imposes only a minimal burden. There is an unfortunate precedent in a 2011 Commerce Department survey of telecom companies on cybersecurity-related issues, where the survey was both complicated and expensive. Congress can help ensure that this experience is not repeated and that requirements are not excessively burdensome.

Congress can also help ensure that in meeting the EO requirement, the Executive Branch collects only the data that will allow it to assess if Framework is effective in improving cybersecurity and where it needs to be amended or strengthened. This essentially revolves around two questions: have companies adopted the framework and is it improving their cybersecurity. Without knowing the answer to these questions, we cannot say if the Framework has improved our defenses against the kinds of actions that affected Anthem, Sony, and many other companies. A simple attestation runs the risk of suffering from what is called in survey research, "respondent error." The best way to reduce the likelihood of this error is to find quantitative metrics that will indicate Framework performance. A quantitative approach is a standard practice in business and should be duplicated in the reports required by the EO.

Over time, it is likely that as companies implement the Framework, their experience will narrow it to a shorter and more focused list of actions relevant to their particular industry sector, as they experiment with different approaches to implementing it. Each industrial sector may find that some parts of the framework are more important for their business than others. An assessment of adoption and effectiveness would speed this evolution and answer important questions about the contributions of the Executive Order and the Framework to better cybersecurity and to national defense.

RESPONSE TO WRITTEN QUESTION SUBMITTED BY HON. BILL NELSON TO DR. JAMES A. LEWIS

Question. NIST is considering the future governance of the Framework so that it is maintained by the private sector instead of by NIST. We have seen with Target, Home Depot, and the numerous other breaches that have occurred in recent years that voluntary industry-maintained standards often do not work. Instead, such industry self-regulation just becomes a minimum standard. And when companies suffer cyberattacks, harming consumers and themselves, they will often just say that they were fully compliant with their respective industry's standards to avoid responsibility for their weak cybersecurity. Do you think there is any danger in that becoming the case for the Framework if it becomes wholly maintained and operated by the private sector?

Answer. The NIST Framework is part of a new approach to cybersecurity created by the February 2013 Executive Order (EO) 13636. It is a voluntary, standards-based approach, reinforced by information sharing, and the involvement of sector specific regulatory agencies. The administration also hopes to identify incentives but any real incentive will probably require legislation.

The involvement of sector specific agencies means that the future development of the Framework will most likely take two separate paths. Sector specific agencies, agencies, in consultation with their critical infrastructure owners and operator partners, will adjust and customize the Framework to better meet the needs of their sectors. At the same time, it is possible that a private entity, such as a non-profit organization will undertake to maintain and update the Framework Document. My understanding is that NIST intends to pass responsibility for updating the Framework to such an entity if it can find a neutral non-profit with sufficient technical expertise.

The EO tasks the sector-specific agencies to work with critical infrastructure owners and operators to maintain and adapt the Framework to their sector's circumstances. This means that future work on the Framework, as part of the larger cybersecurity structure created by EO 13636, will be undertaken as apart of public-private partnerships between critical infrastructure companies and agencies. Since work on the Executive Order began in August 2012, many high-profile incidents have highlighted the need for improved cyber security. Cybersecurity has become an issue of concern for many corporate boards. More incidents can be expected to occur in the future. This heightened attention and increasing risk, along with the government-private sector partnerships, suggests that the impetus will be for these partnerships to improve and extend the Framework and avoid the pitfalls of self-regulation. Congress will have an opportunity to review the status of the Framework and its implementation in September of 2016, since the EO requires agencies to report on implementation, burdensomeness, and effectiveness. This will provide us with data to determine that the framework is actually contributing to better cybersecurity in critical infrastructure or needs to be amended or replaced.

Æ

87

This page intentionally left blank.

88

This page intentionally left blank.

89

This page intentionally left blank.

www.ingramcontent.com/pod-product-compliance
Lightning Source LLC
Chambersburg PA
CBHW081404280526
45788CB00009B/2978

9 781522 954521